at our core

WOMEN WRITING ABOUT POWER

OTHER ANTHOLOGIES FROM
SANDRA HALDEMAN MARTZ

Celebrating Women's Lives
I Am Becoming the Woman I've Wanted
If I Had a Hammer: Women's Work in Poetry, Fiction, and Photographs

Celebrating Aging
When I Am an Old Woman I Shall Wear Purple
If I Had My Life to Live Over I Would Pick More Daisies
Grow Old Along with Me—The Best Is Yet to Be
The Tie That Binds: A Collection of Writings about Fathers &
Daughters / Mothers & Sons

Family Humor
There's No Place Like Home for the Holidays

Also edited by Sandra Haldeman Martz, with images by Deidre Scherer
Threads of Experience

at our core

WOMEN WRITING ABOUT POWER

edited by sandra haldeman martz

Papier-Mache Press
Watsonville, CA

02 01 00 99 98   10 9 8 7 6 5 4 3 2 1

ISBN: 1-57601-007-4 Softcover

Cover art, "Indra" © 1995, by Elly Simmons
Design and composition by Melissa Passehl Design
Editor photograph by Thomas Burke
Copyediting by Cathey S. Cordes
Proofreading by Kim McGinty
Manufactured by Malloy Lithographing, Inc.

Rapping, Elayne, "None of My Best Friends: The Media's Unfortunate 'Victim/Power' Debate," copyright © 1996 by Elayne Rapping. From *"Bad Girls"/"Good Girls": Women, Sex, & Power in the Nineties,* edited by Nan Bauer Maglin and Donna Perry. Reprinted by perission of Rutgers University Press.

Library of Congress Cataloging-in-Publication Data

At our core : women writing about power/edited by Sandra Haldeman Martz.
     p.   cm.
     ISBN 1-57601-007-4 (alk. paper)
     1. Women–Literary collections.   I. Martz, Sandra.
PN6071. W7A86 1998
810.8' 0352042–dc21   97-38219
                                                           CIP

contents

editor's preface

Raised in rural Texas, I grew up surrounded by strong, dependable, solid women: my mother and grandmothers, other farm wives, teachers. In their lives, power was a silent adjective, known but never talked about. Power as a noun—something that could be used—was held by the men: bankers, preachers, school principals, fathers.

Like many children, I didn't look to the real people in my life for inspiration but to the images found on television and in movies, books, and magazines. Early on I wanted to be Heidi or Laura in *Little House on the Prairie*. By the age of twelve, perfection looked like Loretta Young, sweeping down a spiral staircase to greet a room full of loving children. As I entered my teen years, I dreamed of Marlon Brando carrying me away on the back of a Harley. By the time I reached my twenties, I was a single mother, one paycheck away from welfare, and identified more with Janis Joplin's "women is losers." When the 1970s came along, I traded Janis in for Helen Reddy and Gloria Steinem, *Ms.* magazine and *Maude*. Thinking consciously about power for the first time (the term consciousness raising was not accidental), I considered access to education, job opportunities, money, the right to live without fear from abusive mates, and control over my own life.

Throughout the next twenty-five years, enormous change swept through society and individual lives. Newspapers dropped gender classification of jobs. Companies established open job posting systems. Women's leadership was acknowledged at work, in the community, in government. Sexual harassment in the work place was barred and sexual abuse at home was "outed" for the heinous crime it is. Women gained control over their own reproductive systems. Some even accomplished a more balanced division of responsibilities at home. And new media images appeared regularly to show women how powerful we could be.

Several years ago, however, my internal barometer, still fed by the media, began to pick up strange signals. Television sitcoms featured sexual liaisons at the office, illustrating how one party (usually the woman) could use their "power" in these situations to manipulate others. A popular book encouraged married women to give up their jobs and stay home since their incomes didn't significantly exceed the added expenses of child care. Treating others respectfully was transformed into "political correctness," and being PC assured one disdain from colleagues. Women's breasts, mother-in-laws, and blondes once again became fair game for comedians. On the hard news side, newspaper reporting on women's issues and female public figures began to decline, and a fifteen-year trend narrowing the gap between median earnings for men and women was reversed.

Such signs of the erosion of women's power inspired this project. I wanted to know what other women thought about power, how they defined it. Did they feel powerful now and how had that changed over time? Did they want more power in their lives and, if so, what would they be willing to do to get it? How would they use that power?

After two years of reading—more than four thousand submissions including philosophical observations in the accompanying cover letters and feedback from my network of women friends and colleagues—I don't have definitive answers but I am more intrigued than ever with the questions.

From these sources, I learned that many women (far too many) do not feel powerful in their personal lives. Their solutions to the imbalance of power in their relationships often involve ending the relationship and sometimes include violence, real or imagined, especially in reaction to physical abuse. The sheer volume of writing about abusive male/female relationships was almost overwhelming. A few women spoke of power struggles with other women, but they were much more likely to cite the support they received from other women.

Women often tied power to learning and education. Several wrote of power achieved through overcoming difficult circumstances; many saw themselves on the brink of becoming more powerful and acknowledged the freedom of closing "old doors" in order to open up new ones of opportunity. They saw self-reliance as a path to increased power, but they also celebrated the power of women in community. Many envisioned using their power to do more for others. Intuition, the ability to nurture and heal, and creativity were often cited as examples of women's power. Most women expected to grow more powerful with age, but spiritual power seemed important to women in all age groups. A surprising number of the writers used fantasy and magical realism to depict women in more powerful positions.

Few women addressed public or political power: economic power, control over systems and resources, power over others, or organized resistance to abusive power systems. Women more often talked about ways to work around the system rather than using direct confrontation. Those who did focus on political power tended to be activists, veterans of the '70s feminist movement, or both.

Narrowing the material down to a book-length collection was, as always, very difficult. In the selections, women's power is sometimes an overt player, as in Sharon Nelson's look at women writers in "Silencing"; sometimes it is more subtle as in Mary Kelly's "The Long Night" where the power of friendship transcends even death.

Sexuality is explored as both a source of power as in Janice Eidus's "Gypsy Lore," and a source of potential abuse as in May-lee Chai's "The Dancing Girl's Story." There's laughter (feminists do have a sense of humor) in Joan Zimmerman's look at "Eve," resolution of anger in "The Glass-Smashing Wall" by Pam Burris (sorry readers, it's a fictional wall that should exist somewhere but doesn't yet), and spiritual celebration in Judy Lightwater's "winter solstice." Fifty-six stories and poems and fifteen photographs paint a compelling tale, rich and complex with images that will stay with you for a long time.

Because I believe the media continues to exert a far-reaching influence on both our individual perspectives and the organizational and institutional infrastructures that nurture or oppress our expression of power, I wanted to provide a larger context for reading these creative works. I greatly admire the work of Elayne Rapping, feminist media critic and professor of communication at Adelphi University, whom I first encountered through her columns in *On the Issues*. Her practical and thoughtful insights always seemed to speak to the same audience I wanted to reach through our anthology series celebrating women's lives: real women trying to make sense out of complex issues while they tend to the business of living.

Elayne's essay, reprinted from *"Bad Girls"/"Good Girls": Women, Sex, & Power in the Nineties* (Rutgers University Press, 1996), challenges the media polarization of the issue of women and power into two camps—powerbabes vs. crybabies—and provides a historical and analytical look at how women are portrayed in the media. She reminds us all that we have the power to challenge these oversimplified stereotypes and apply our own clear thinking to the issues.

My deepest gratitude goes to Elayne Rapping, to the thousands of women and the handful of men who submitted work to this project, to the sixty-two women whose work is offered here, to my dedicated, hardworking staff who support me so well through these explorations, especially Shirley Coe, and to the wonderful women friends and colleagues who keep me honest and striving for integrity. More power to you!

—SANDRA HALDEMAN MARTZ

none of my best friends: the media's unfortunate "victim/power" debate

ELAYNE RAPPING

Victims and victors; winners and losers; crybabies and powerhouses. Who are these media-constructed cartoon characters we are supposed to be these days? When I agreed to contribute to this volume, I thought I knew what it all meant and where I stood on the battlefield. But the more I thought about it, the more confused I became. Of course I don't agree with the many recent pronouncements by women who should know better about how much power women have in these post-feminist days: how sexual violence is no longer a problem; how women today can just buy or shout our way into high places; how those who are beaten down by gender oppression should simply pick themselves up by their Bruno Magli bootstraps—easily charged with their gold cards—and get a hot new "power" life, as advertised in *Elle.*

So I guess I belong on the other team, with all the victims and losers and terminally good girls who are stuck behind the economic and emotional eight ball; suffering helplessly the slings and arrows of male aggression and injustice; and responding with self-destructive addictions or—in moments of sheer desperation and "temporary insanity"—hysteria and violence.

Neither of these team uniforms—the Dolce and Gabbana or the sackcloth and ashes—suits me. Neither description has much to do with the world I actually live in and the women I actually know. So what gives? Ain't I a feminist?

Brain amuddle, desk piled high with either/or books and articles, I turned in desperation to a videotape of a television movie I had not yet had the courage to watch—*Tonya and Nancy: The Inside Story*—in the hopes that the media, which, after all, has been fueling the whole debate, would know what it was supposed to mean. But, like me (although with far less taste and intelligence) NBC was confused. The writers, producers, and actors were as clueless as I about who was supposed to be the victim and who the powerbabe. Of course they understood that Nancy Kerrigan, well-groomed, polite, from a loving, all-American family—and after all the one who was kneecapped—was, by definition, a victim. That made her—according to the guidelines set down by Camille Paglia and Katie Roiphe and Naomi Wolf and the rest—the "good girl" to Tonya Harding's "bad girl," the smoking, cussing, truck-driving sexpot from the wrong side of the tracks.

Except that by movie's end, Nancy was clearly the powerhouse—the "go-for-it!", endorsement-rich, multimillionaire winner. And Tonya, the darling of many feminists who want to see women represented as powerful and aggressive, had somehow devolved into a textbook version of the female "victim," physically, sexually, and emotionally abused and dominated by her mother, her stepbrother, and her bullying, manipulating thug of a husband.

As dumb and tacky as this movie was, I had to admit that its confusion about victim/power gender issues was not all that different from my own. And the reason, I finally realized, was that the terms of the debate had very little to do with feminist goals or values, as I understand them. My own feelings about Tonya and Nancy were indeed confused because I liked and disliked, rooted for and abhorred, both of them. Both were strong, accomplished fighters for "power." And both were also exploited "victims" of the crass money- and power-driven male world which had pitted them against each other in a public battle for a nearly unattainable "victory" tainted by greed, phoniness, and ruthless competition. Was either version the Cinderella story I would wish young girls to be guided by in their quests for success and happiness in these post-feminist times? Would I want my daughter or my students to be obsessively dreaming and then elbowing their ways toward such endlessly out-of-reach, politically suspect goals? No way.

Still, the movie was instructive. In this media spectacle of Tonya vs. Nancy—the sickeningly sweet good girl against the bitchy, greedy bad girl—there is, I think, a paradigm of what is wrong and self-defeating in this current, media-fueled debate about what kind of "feminism" we should be practicing or endorsing. Both options assume some things we second-wave feminists never assumed when we began our struggle to free ourselves from sexist culture. First, that the system itself, in which power is defined in terms of mercenary, individualistic values, would be taken as a given. And second, that those who still, for whatever reasons, had not managed to overcome the emotional and political barriers that were keeping them down, would—until the revolution—be considered losers, victims, hopeless zeros. The power feminists certainly do imply that the basic system and its values are just fine and all we need to do is reach out and grab a piece of the pie.

The class and race blindness of this position is glaring, offensive, and easily refuted. Of course most women—all but the few who do indeed wear Gucci, carry gold cards, and appear in bookstore windows, on op-ed pages, and in slick magazines—are in no position to "go for it!" They are, indeed, beaten down, still, by economic, social, and emotional oppression. And because of the importance of reminding the world of this key factor in the gender wars—of the very real suffering and inequity that still inform most women's existences (Katie Roiphe, Naomi Wolf, and their friends notwithstanding)—we are apt to sound as though we are, indeed, arguing that women as a whole are hopelessly victimized and enslaved by sexism.

But this either/or posing of the matter is way too simplistic. Wrong and infuriating as the power women are in their glib smugness, it is no good to simply reply, implicitly or explicitly, that they are *all* wrong, that because we have not yet gotten as far as these others claim in our quest for power and success, we have somehow stayed exactly where we were at the beginning. The fact is that there is a grain of truth in the power rhetoric that we ought to acknowledge and claim as our own, even as we refute the many flip falsities upon which the bulk of it is based.

Feminism, as a political force, has indeed brought some radical and significant changes to the realm of gender relations. Of course these changes are only a beginning, do not always work to make individual women's lives better, and are met with an understandable backlash of rage and fear by the male power structure. Nonetheless, the arena in which we began our struggle thirty years ago looks and feels a lot different today because of our efforts. To quote Martin Luther King, shortly before his death, "We aren't where we *want* to be. And we aren't where we're *going* to be. But we sure are a long way from where we *were*."

UTOPIA REVISITED

If we go back to the beginning of the second wave and recall our original vision and purpose, we can perhaps better see the reductiveness of the current debate and its historic and political confusions. In the 1960s, when we began our struggle, we were driven by two powerful insights. First, we suddenly understood—as though the scales had fallen from our eyes—that our personal and social circumstances had been largely determined by the masculinist institutions and ideas by which we were forced to live. Suddenly, so much of our misery, failure, and powerlessness appeared to us in their true colors, as effects of a politically unjust culture and society.

And so we set about to transform these institutions, to free ourselves from our powerlessness by creating a brave new world, a revolutionary new social order. Our dream of a radically democratic, feminist victory—like so much of the rhetoric of the New Left and counterculture—was wildly, deliriously utopian and optimistic. That was its weakness perhaps. But it also had a great strength. It kept us focused on a broad vision of social transformation, which, if unrealistic, was useful as a reminder of the scope of what we were trying to achieve and how hard and complicated and long would be the struggle.

Perhaps most important, the grandiosity of our utopian visions allowed us to see, as it seems so hard to do today, that one might indeed be a victim—of so many male forces—and yet, at the same time, become more and more empowered, personally and as a collective entity, through political struggle. But of course, back then, we never assumed that we were talking about individual women in isolation from all other women, in all other places and conditions. Naively, as the now widely understood problem of "difference" among women makes clear, we assumed that one could generalize about "women" as if all of us were more or less in the same place in the gender wars, suffering the same problems in the same degree, and desiring the same kinds of solutions to the same kinds of suffering.

We now know that this is nonsense; that the norms we thought applied to all women actually were typical, mostly, of white middle-class Western women. Indeed, it is one of the most serious of the blind spots of the power feminists that they are persisting in this naively narcissistic vision of feminist revolution as white, Western, and middle-class. But recognizing the "difference" problem, and the complications it brings to our project of collective feminist revolution, does not negate the progress we have made in many areas. It simply reminds us that these victories are partial and unstable. That they exist as part of a much larger, darker mosaic of shifting power struggles in which "winning" and "losing" are far more ambiguous terms than we originally, naively, assumed.

The grandiosity of our vision, naive as it was, provided us with a second political insight which gave historic perspective to our project. Starting from zero, as it then seemed we were, we were likely to see our struggle in terms of a dominant narrative in which victimization and empowerment coexisted as two necessary terms in a full equation of "women's liberation." Of course we were victims; and of course—and this was exciting—we were every day empowering ourselves, in small and large ways, individually and collectively, as we worked to change the terms and conditions of our lives.

This boldly utopian narrative is still, I think, the most powerful and accurate way of talking about the gender wars. We are still, inevitably, victimized in many ways. And we are still in the process of changing that fact. Two or three decades after we began our war against patriarchy, it is meaningless to ask if we have "won" or "lost." We are all, together and individually, at varying stages of struggle. We are, in truth, still victims of capitalism and patriarchy. And we are all, insofar as we partake of the fruits of feminist struggle, consciously or not, more powerful than when we began.

The problem, it often seems to me, is that we have allowed the mainstream media to lead us into a falsely binary, an either/or trap in which we are either terminally imprisoned or miraculously "free at last!" As a media critic, someone who regularly comments publicly upon the state of gender representation in popular culture, I am aware of the ease with which one may fall into this trap. It is possible, the easiest thing in the world actually, to view the media's portrayal of women as wholly reactionary—a monolith of misogyny, even on its best days. One may read a given text—*Thelma and Louise* or *The Accused* let's say—and focus only on those places where male hegemony exerts its ultimate power, as of course it always will, until Procter and Gamble, Mobil Oil, and the Bank of America are put out of business.

And it is also possible to read the media only in terms of what's changed and improved for women. From Donna Reed to Mary Richards to Murphy Brown is, after all, more than a few steps in a feminist direction. From Tammy Wynette to Emmylou Harris to k.d. lang is at least as many steps toward freedom and autonomy. From *Dirty Harry* and *The Wild Bunch* to *Thelma and Louise* and *The Accused* is a good long feminist stride across the silver screen. Indeed, while those who watch less television than I may be shocked to hear it, one could fill a very huge volume with examples of how and where the media have indeed been forced to adopt and incorporate progressive gender images and ideas—in soap operas, sitcoms, docudramas, and daytime talk shows, especially.

But neither of these ploys—while they make for neat little Sunday arts-and-leisure columns—is fair or accurate in its assessment of how we are doing, overall, in the struggle to change gender representation and discourse. It is far more useful, I think, to see the media themselves as an arena of political struggle in which—over three decades and on a daily, hourly basis—we are collectively working to change the reactionary conventions which have for so long dominated our culture. Sometimes we win; mostly we lose. Sometimes our victories are thrown back in our faces. Sometimes they manage to stay put and engender more victories against the grain of masculinist resistance. All in all, it's an inconclusive, but dynamic and energizing picture. Except we rarely view it "all in all."

Looking back over my own recent columns and reviews, for example, I am struck by my own almost zany inconsistencies. Day by day, movie by movie, news story by news story, I am apt to sound wildly Pollyanna-ish on some days and suicidally hopeless on others. *Thelma and Louise*, Liz Phair and the Breeders, *Roseanne*, and *Murphy Brown* (flawed as they all must be in places) seem to me cause for champagne and roses, hard-won victories for our side. The Academy Awards, Rush Limbaugh and Howard Stern, Snoop Doggy Dog and Sir Mix-a-Lot; the trashing of Amy Fisher and Lorena Bobbitt seem to affirm my worst fears: that we have gotten nowhere at all, or worse, been pushed backward by the Neanderthals.

But, as the most interesting female media figures make clear, the truth is muddier. The progress, the small grabs at power and authority, are always in the context of the original victimization we are continually trying to overcome. And the victimization—now that feminism has so politicized and called attention to it—is always in the context of a now-taken-for-granted struggle to empower, the very existence of which is itself a triumph, given where we started from.

Lorena Bobbitt—to use one of many media-driven gender tales which dominated public consciousness for quite a while—most certainly was a victim, one with no designer bootstraps handy with which to pull herself out of her tragic trap. But, because of feminism's success in politicizing that victimization, her act of desperation was read and analyzed by everyone—rightists and leftists alike—in feminist terms, as a political tale. Alone, Lorena Bobbitt was a desperate victim. But she was not alone in the aftermath of her action. She was hurled into a collective tale of female resistance and empowerment and became—to her surprise, perhaps—part of the historic narrative to which I refer. In this case, as in so many others, victimization and empowerment, personal and political narratives, are symbiotically intertwined, because feminism, as a historic force, exists and thrives.

Roseanne, whose own relationship to media is fascinating in its complexity, provides an even more interesting example of how impossible and foolish it is to try to separate victimization from empowerment in today's gendered world. On the one hand, Roseanne is undoubtedly one of the ones who have "made it," a powerbabe if ever there was one. She is, after all, one of the most powerful women in the media, the creator and controller of a show that has gone further toward overturning the sexist conventions of pop culture than any other I can think of. In that sense, surely, she has beaten the media at their sexist games, both economically and culturally.

But Roseanne is also a self-identified victim of many things, not only in the past, but now, at the height of her success, as she herself is only too willing to tell the world. And even within the representational world of media images, she is hardly home free in her battle with the boys at the top. For every radically transgressive episode of *Roseanne* she manages to push past the sponsors, the FCC, and the Standards and Practices guys, there are—in the tabloids, in stand-up comedy clubs, in news headlines and magazine features—at least a dozen far less flattering images of Roseanne in which she is, still, the butt of the worst kind of sexist degradation, exploitation, and humiliation. Such are the contradictions of any moment of success for women in a male world. We are always losing and winning, kicking butt and getting trashed, all at the same time, in both our personal and political lives.

And so it goes as we feminists argue among ourselves and with the powers that be over how we are doing and what label we can safely wear in public. "What about Madonna?" we continue to wonder, in academic journals, with each other, and on op-ed pages. Is she a feminist heroine or a throwback to the most retrograde images? She certainly places herself in the power camp, and with justification. She has, to her credit, gone a long way toward overturning the sexual double standard and offering a model of female confidence and empowerment which has been an inspiration to bad girls everywhere, and she's put a few ideas in the heads of a lot of good ones, too.

But, although I am a fan, I can understand why many are troubled by her glib way of putting herself and her sexualized appearance and behavior forth as realistic possibilities for women to safely imitate. For, as her critics point out, the many young girls who do imitate her dress and style are likely to be met in the real world with a male public very much in the dark about the liberatory intent of Madonna's work; men who still think she and her wannabes look and act a lot like the retro images of women in *Playboy* and *Hustler* who seem (to them) to be "asking for it."

In fact, the flip side of Madonna's very healthy and radical way of twisting the terms and conventions of sexist culture to show how they would look and feel if women were in power is probably Amy Fisher, a young girl whose own life may well have been modeled on her impression of what celebrities like Madonna can now get away with, even prosper with and thrive on. And yet, in Fisher's own life and in the media version of that life, she became, in acting the powerful, sexy, bad girl, one of the most pathetic victims of misogyny in recent history. The legal professionals, the network docudrama and tabloid producers, the writers and publishers, the men who abused and exploited her personally throughout her life, every one of them made a killing by using her body and her life in the most viciously sexist ways. And not even the women's movement, I'm sorry to say, was there to say a political word in her behalf as she was taken to prison while her boyfriend partied with Donald Trump.

This kind of thing does not happen to Madonna in her videos and concerts (although we don't know what might happen to her in her personal dealings with actual men). It doesn't, we hear, happen to Katie Roiphe or Camille Paglia or Naomi Wolf, either. They are too powerful, they would have us believe. But this victimization surely did happen to poor Amy Fisher, on-screen, in print, and in life. Just as it happens every day to other nameless, faceless, book-contractless women.

So what is going on here? Do we say that Roseanne and Madonna are losers still? Do we credit them with no power because—personally and professionally—they and their progressive media efforts are still inevitably hampered and mitigated by the strong arm of male power? Is Madonna not a winner unless Amy Fisher, is too? Is Roseanne only the sum of her weaknesses and failures, not her successes?

This way of posing the question is, again, falsely dichotomized and reductive. Certainly, and most important, we must always remind ourselves and each other that the ultimate power imbalance is still vast and will continue to be, certainly during our lifetimes. That white, straight, rich American men do indeed control and manipulate most of the institutions by which we live. And that all this talk of "power" feminism is disingenuous and self-serving.

But having said that—and we have been saying it for three decades—it is also necessary, on occasion, to take stock of what the playing field now looks like and tally up the places where we have indeed chipped away a bit at male hegemony and power, made a few dents in their chrome-and-mahogany surfaces, even when, at the moment of battle, it may have seemed as if we were getting trounced. For the final judgment of an event can never be made at the moment of impact, when one's perspective is necessarily limited.

As a case in point, an illustration of how complex and confusing single, freeze-frame, moment-in-time cases can be, let's look at one final example: The AnitaHill/Clarence Thomas episode, as it played at the time and as it looks today. The initial public reactions to Anita Hill's foray into national prominence, by feminists and nonfeminists alike, were largely depressed and depressing. "We lost," said almost everyone I knew, at the time of Thomas's confirmation. Hill was vilified and humiliated, disbelieved by most Americans, even women. And Thomas is now a Supreme Court justice.

And yet, several years down the road, Hill's place in American history seems destined to loom far larger and more significantly than Thomas's. For, in the grand scheme of things, victories come slowly and in such small steps we are often incapable of seeing them. And the scars we bear in the process of winning are often so painful as to feel like defeat and humiliation.

As, in many ways, they are. In the wake of the hearings more battles ensued—Tailhook, most prominently—in which we have often fared very badly, indeed. But amidst these headline-making sexual harassment cases, there are myriad others which may never get media play but in which we are gaining ground. No one of these cases is definitive. But together they represent an enormously important political assault on male power. For what ultimately matters is that today, as a result of Hill's courage and integrity, sexual harassment as an issue is hotly and continuously contested in every major arena of public life, from the courts to the military to the corporate world to the media. And every man, even the president of the United States, has felt the chill wind of its ominous message.

In the big picture of public life, then, there are no individual battles, no final winners or losers. Madonna and Amy Fisher, Anita Hill and Lani Guinier, are all in the same game. So are Tonya and Nancy. So are Lorena Bobbitt and Thelma and Louise. So, even, are Zoe Baird and her au pair girl. And none of them, not even Zoe or Madonna, has totally escaped the bounds of sexist oppression. Sure, they are winners compared to most of us. So are Camille and Katie and Naomi. But they are also, still, victims of a sexist world—even if they don't admit it—in which the double standards, the scars of socialization, the indignities of male power structures, keep them that much further down the ladder they breathlessly climb than their male counterparts.

In such a world, at such a confusing, indeterminate point in history, I am unwilling to cede the "power" words to the "powerbabes" or to retreat—and so accept *their* terms and narratives—to the "victim" position which sees loss and failure as the definitive condition of women today. I don't buy it. Child of the 1960s that I am, I insist on reminding myself and everyone else I can get to listen, of that original utopian blueprint—now updated with much raw data about class, race, sexual, and national difference—upon which we cut our political teeth. In that early narrative, admitting our own current victimizations and failures and pains was *not* a negative, but a positive thing, a first exciting step toward empowerment—for ourselves and for those who listened and heard and joined us in the struggle to overcome. That is still the point of a political struggle of any kind, after all: to recognize our common pain and disempowerment and struggle, through all the ups and downs and wins and losses that actual social change demands, to change the world so that such things will not happen in the future—the distant future, not the one on next week's cover of *Time* or tomorrow's op-ed page.

at our core

WOMEN WRITING ABOUT POWER

Photo by Margaret Randall

silencing

FOR ELIZABETH BARRETT BROWNING, EDNA
ST. VINCENT MILLAY, DOROTHY PARKER,
SYLVIA PLATH, ET ALIA

I

A WOMAN WRITER, SIMPLY BY VIRTUE OF BEING A WOMAN AND A WRITER,
IS A RENEGADE AND A SUBVERSIVE, YET WE READ WOMEN'S WRITING
AS IF IT HAD BEEN WRITTEN BY RESPECTABLE MEN.

My mothers who are lost have been denied
their majority. They are not Major Figures.
They lie uneasy in narrow graves
fitted to contain them narrowly.

They do not take
so much space
as a man.

If you listen carefully, you will hear them.
They stalk, clanking their bracelets and bones.
They scream, laugh and tell jokes, are ribald and bitchy.
They grin widely, reveal imperfect teeth.
They smack their thighs. They cackle, crackle,
crack their knuckles, tighten their hands into fists.

Their lines spill out, spill over, spill forth, released
like bellies from girdles, midriffs from stays,
thighs from the tight lines of garter belts. They are released
from the tyranny of pantyhose, from speaking Prose.

My mothers who are lost stamp their lines in rhythm,
spit words out of books in all directions,
commit the sin of inelegance. They are noisy as an army.

My mothers who are lost scream at us.
Nothing is sacred to them. They will not be stilled.
They are in pain. Their pain is visible, tangible,
woven into words that betray it. They tell us:

We have been here before you, my dears;
we know the score.
We know the meanings of "Literature,"
the convenient historiographic lies that obtrude
so that when we speak clearly,
what we say cannot be heard.

The study of Literature,
a bloated politics of meaning,
prevents you from seeing;
biographical detail stops you from hearing;
and history, the cloak of those who define
the growth of their own power over time,
is murderous in its uses;
like cotton wool stuffed in a mouth or down a throat,
innocuous in itself, nursery furnishing,
it chokes our voices as it blocks your ears.

My mothers who are lost are impatient.
They scream at us, scream their stories,
scream a warning, scream the lesson,
scream the answer to the riddle.

They scream the pain:
You're getting fucked,
fucked over,
fucked by form.

II

IF A WRITER DOES NOT PRODUCE WHAT IS CONSISTENT
WITH THE IDEOLOGY OF THE DOMINANT CULTURE,
NO ONE WILL HEAR HER VOICE.
IF A WRITER PRODUCES WHAT IS CONSISTENT
WITH THE IDEOLOGY OF THE DOMINANT CULTURE,
SHE MAY CHOKE ON HER OWN WORDS.

I contemplate their narrow graves,
the narrower grave prepared for me,
contraction of the female form to fit
a narrow shelf,
contraction of the voice to fit
constriction of the soul.

Form is a matter of fashion
like the length of skirts,
the wearing of business suits,
the bustle, the doublet, the tie,
kohl or mascara to darken an eye;
and content is
what those who write history
determine it to be or to have been,
the clear meanings poets strive for
lost in the war
that is won neither by poetry nor politics
but by force.

The brain's a squishy thing in its breakable carapace,
contains the fear we live with,
our own physical death.

We endure
the wounding and maiming
the shaping
to form
forming, reforming
to the meanest of meanings
to live.

And who would tell us no?

Constricted, contracted,
shrunk and shriven,
we make what is pleasing,
what makes us pleasing,
what we form to be pleasing
and what forms us to be pleasing
however it mis-shapes us
so that we take the smallest spaces,
speak in the smallest voices,
barely audible,
sometimes
not audible at all.

searching for a woman's name

Crawling within
some abandoned shell,
tracing the whorls that lead to the core,
whorls like the ones
on my mother's hands,
my own,
I am spiraling
past the names of fathers, grandfathers,
down through the opalescent sea
where the names must be—there
where the roaring begins.

6   P h o t o b y M a r g a r e t R a n d a l l

wise woman's friend gets interviewed about how the power begins

sure she's a little
different always was
the smallest kid in her class

looks into things
the way a needle slides
clean through scarlet silk

climbed a roof once
where the stars shot gold
into her sixteen years

I've heard her sing
on a stage with no one
able to reach her voice

she's pepper on bread
she's rain in December
she's hair that curls beyond curl

catch her dancing
some silent Sunday:
she'll spin your blood to joy

call

There is a new sound
of roaring voices in the deep
and light-shattered rushes in the heavens.
The mountains are coming alive,
the fire-kindled mountains
moving again to reshape the earth.
It is we sleeping women
waking up in a darkened world,
cutting the chains from off our bodies
with our teeth,
stretching our lives over the slow earth,
seeing, moving, breathing in the vigor
that commands us to make all things new.

It has been said that while the women sleep
the earth shall sleep.
But listen! We are waking up and rising,
and soon our sister will know her strength.
The earth-moving day is here.
We women wake to move in fire.
The earth shall be remade.

the dream catcher

"Doña Rosa is a *bruja*," I say. "A witch."

My mother slaps me, then makes the sign of the cross.

"She's got a mustache," I say and duck under the table.

My mother pounds tortillas. She hands me the good dishes and points with her nose. I place doña Rosa's teacup upside down and poke a hole through her napkin.

"Ay, Virgencita," my mother sighs, straightening the lace doilies under the statues of the Virgen de Guadalupe. She prays for me to grow up right and be a proper señorita, without killing her first with worry. My mother says I will wear myself out as well, that too much wanting is not good.

"Resígnate," she says. "Accept things as they are, Charito." She says I do not need to be the best, the first, the strongest.

Over the years her collection of statues has grown. Countless candles have been lit.

My mother once tried to scare me with tales of *La Llorona,* who drowned her children, then ran off with her lover. She showed me pictures of the ugly crone, dressed in black, who prowled the riverbanks. When it rained at night, the howling wind was said to be the suffering of *La Llorona,* being punished by Dios for her sins.

"Watch out," my mother said. *"La Llorona* kidnaps *niños* who misbehave."

But, when the sky was at its darkest, I waited at the riverbank with a flashlight. A black figure arose, with a light blinking above its head. I ran toward a moaning, whining sound. What happened next was kind of blurry, as if my head were being held under water, or as if it were passing through a cloud. Pressure on my chest, fingers pinching my nose, and this smell, this terrible smell. I jumped like a frog, belching out water until puddles slapped at my feet. I opened my hand and a square of black cloth glowed and zipped into the sky like a shooting star.

"Mamá," I said. "I held her power. Here in my hand."

Padre Martín said I had smelled the charred bodies at the entrance of hell. When I left confession, I spun in four directions, raised my arms and called down a rainstorm.

Only doña Rosa could explain the rash on my palm and the black eyes I gave to my classmates. She placed pennies soaked in *agua bendita* on my forehead, balanced lit candles on the coins, and covered them with a glass.

"I held her power," I repeated.

"No, Charito," doña Rosa said. "She held yours."

When my mother was pregnant with me, she caught the *mal de ojo,* the evil eye, from a jealous woman whose husband was sterile. I was born a month early, one nostril pinched, my lips twisted in a sneer. Doña Rosa hung a garlic wreath over my crib, then snipped and poked and bathed me in scented water. She untwisted my lips, but left a scar. To remind me, she told my mother, that what came easy in life did not count.

"Doña Rosa is a busy woman," my mother says now, boiling water for tea. She touches the scar above my lip. "You should be thankful she has offered her help again."

"Even Papá thinks doña Rosa's a witch," I say.

"What did you tell him?" My mother grips my elbow.

"Nada," I shrug and make my eyes go blank. I think of La Lolita and the mangos she threw in my mother's face while my father swore none of it was true.

Doña Rosa's advice was written on heart-shaped paper dipped in cologne. Mamá took my father's sock and stuffed it with two *bolillos* from the bakery. The birds pecked at the sock, their beaks breaking through to the hard rolls inside. The ants carried away bits of its soft middle dough. My father lost his energy. His shoulders slumped. His pants sagged. La Lolita came with a sack and dumped my father's clothes on our porch.

When doña Rosa learned the news, she whispered, "Illusion is the first of all powers." Then she scratched my scar with her thumbnail.

Now the front door opens. My mother hugs doña Rosa, her words coming out in one breath.

"It's Charito." My mother pushes me forward. "For two weeks she has roamed the house in her sleep, banging on the walls, her words turned inside out. Last night she stood on the porch and screamed." Doña Rosa smokes a cigar. Her head is wrapped in a red bandanna.

"Take your shoes off," she says. "Bad spirits leave through your feet."

I throw my shoes over my shoulder without looking. My mother hushes me with her eyes.

Doña Rosa flicks ashes on the floor. The tip of her pinkie is missing. "You must sleep with the windows closed and your bedroom door locked. Dreams can turn into smoke, float out the window, and be dreamt by someone else. Good dreams can be stolen. And the bad ones," doña Rosa inhales deeply, "why be responsible for the nightmares of a stranger?"

I watch my toes wiggle until my mother clears her throat. "Tell me your dreams." Doña Rosa's voice is husky. "Spirits often dance with another's desires."

My mother bites her lip. Her hand shakes as she pours tea.

I fold my arms over my chest and tighten my lips. Doña Rosa grabs my chin with her hand. She stares into my eyes and pops the secrets from my skin as if piercing a boil with a steaming cloth. She snatches at them and curls her fingers, one by one, squeezing, squeezing, her eyes dark knots in her face. Then slowly she stretches out her fingers and rubs her palm down her thigh. Her eyes become calm and empty, like the unblinking stare of a cow. Stripped of my secrets, I feel weak and chilled.

"Now we are ready to begin," she says and wraps her shawl around my shoulders. Doña Rosa reaches into her bag and pulls out a red candle. She lights it with the tip of her cigar, then waves it above my head.

I take a step backward and feel a wind behind my knees. My voice sounds hollow, the words shifting slowly, like wet sand.

"I am in a car—"

"In the backseat," doña Rosa interrupts. "You are not in control. Who is driving?"

"A man with a hat—"

"You see only the back of his head," she says. "He doesn't talk, but his power reaches you from miles away."

"The car is speeding—"

"You have big hopes."

"We are going down a road—"

"That is bumpy," doña Rosa says. "Your future is filled with highs and lows." Her hands move like waves.

"In the backseat are rats and they—"

"Bite you," doña Rosa shows her teeth. "They chew on your shoes. Something is eating your soul."

"We see a house on a hill."

"It is your spirit. You travel up and up, but it is out of reach."

"As I try to get out," I say, "the car slips backward. We fall down the hill—"

"So fast you can't breathe. You climb over into the driver's seat to grab the steering wheel." Doña Rosa makes a fist.

"But I can't hold it. It burns my fingers. Then I wake up."

Doña Rosa lights another cigar and closes her eyes. The room is like a grey cloud. I cough and my mother steps on my foot.

Doña Rosa touches the delicate webs hanging from the bulb above her head. "See the spider? It's web is the circle of life. She grows older and wiser, spinning faster and stronger. The web gets bigger, yet a hole is always left in its center."

Doña Rosa reaches into her bag. She takes out a metal hoop strung with feathers, bells and beads. "This is a dream catcher," she says. "Hang it over your bed and it will sift your dreams. Good dreams will pass through the center hole. Evil thoughts will be trapped to perish in the light of dawn. Now, your dreams will lead you where you want to go."

Doña Rosa tightens the bandanna around her head. She kisses my mother on the cheek. *"Él que adelante no mira, atrás se queda.* Not to look ahead is to stay behind. Charito will be fine. You must let her do—so you can be." She erases the frown from my mother's forehead.

Doña Rosa's eyelids look as papery as petals pressed in a book. She places her hand over my heart. "Your power," she says. "It comes from here."

My mother walks doña Rosa to the door. "*Sueña con los angelitos,*" doña Rosa calls to me. "Dream with the angels."

After doña Rosa leaves, I clench my fists and feel my muscles tighten. My heart beats as if I have run with the wind. I stare through my mother's back until she turns around.

"Mamá?" I say.

My mother doesn't answer. She closes the kitchen windows. Then she gets a hammer and takes the hoop from my hand. Our laughter flies up into the air and wraps itself around each of us like rings of smoke.

runoff

Ten minutes before lunch, ten weeks before summer. Penmanship lesson drones on and on, endless loops and dips and just-so slanted, just-so tall, just-so long, over and around and endlessly again the useless practice of perfection. We must learn these things so that we are employable when we are adults, we must be employable so that we can make money, we must make money so that we can eat. As senseless and useless an argument as the practice of handwriting. Did they mean to tell us so early in life that the purpose of life was to eat, or rather to not go hungry?

Mrs. Greames says that I may go to the pencil sharpener. I walk as slowly as I dare, as though walking in the lake, to prolong this opportunity for physical movement. If I can make it last ten full minutes, just ten eternal minutes, the lesson will be over and it will be time for lunch. Time for the purpose of living.

The thick chemical stink of processed leather from Felton's Tannery blows across the street and into the gaping window in front of me. It saturates the classroom air. Mrs. Greames left the classroom twice this morning with a handkerchief over her nose and mouth. She's not from around here. I am. The smell reminds me of Grandpa and for a minute I think he's across the street, working at the factory right now, instead of dead.

"Tracy, get away from the window and take your seat. *Please.*" Nobody else in the world calls me Tracy. I've been called Track practically since I was born. Mrs. Greames says Track is not a lady's name. She places a lot of importance on being a lady. She always says *please*, always says *thank you*. It's one of her rules. I wonder why it's not in her rules to say it nicely.

"I'm sharpening my pencil, Mrs. Greames." I jam my pencil in the pencil sharpener and turn the crank hard and fast. The point breaks off, so I can stand here longer.

Mrs. Greames hardly ever teaches us anything. The only time she uses the blackboard is to list all her silly rules. I heard Mama tell Grandma that they transferred Mrs. Greames to our school to try and force her to retire. She despises this school; she despises us.

The school is more than a hundred years old. A fire trap, Grandma says. Its foundation rises steeply, maybe thirty feet, above Seawall Street—we call it "Sewer Street." The street is one of three narrow, uneven alleys that connect our neighborhood to Main Street. An old brook runs under the street, catching the runoff from Felton's Tannery.

When it rains the brook overflows. Sewer Street becomes a deep, swirling, purple and green river that shines like rainbows when the sun hits it. We line our bicycles up at the top of the hill and take turns plowing through it. If your bike is big enough and you can get up enough speed, you can send rainbows sailing into the air on both sides of you. I usually wipe out in the deepest part.

The windows of the school are wide and screenless. To open and close them, we use a long stick, the length of four brooms, fitted with a heavy brass hook on one end. If I stood on the broad pine windowsill right now and spread my arms, my fingers would still not touch the window frames.

I yearn to do this, to lean forward and be sucked out into the wide grey sky, the stench and clouds holding me afloat. I'm moving by sheer intention through the air, across the school yard, over the fence, down to the tannery. I'm pausing at the second window from the left, fourth floor, where Grandpa worked tacking hides. If I can fly, Grandpa can still be alive. He's glancing up from his tacking board. I'm waving to him. Delight is pressing through his sweaty face. "That's my grand-daughter, you know," he's saying to Joe and Mickey, the other tackers in the room. They are astonished. Mickey is unconsciously raising his hand to his forehead to bless himself. Grandpa's not astonished, just proud.

I hear her before I see her, and it pulls me right out of the sky, away from my daydream. I look down into the school yard. There's my sister, Jody, sitting on the warm tarmac, wailing. The other second graders play around her like she's not even there. Two teachers lean on the back of Mr. Conway's Buick at the other end of the yard, talking. They don't even glance over at her.

Lately Jody has been having these ferocious crying fits. Mama says she's just being dramatic. Grandma says it's from eating too many sweets. Her teacher, Miss Murray, says nothing; she doesn't even care. They all think she can stop. But she can't. The wailing just takes her over. That's what they don't understand.

"Mrs. Greames, I have to go outside and take care of my sister." It is against the rules to speak out loud without raising your hand.

"Tracy, sit down. *Please.* Miss Murray will take care of her."

Just then I hear Jody sobbing louder. I know from experience that she's not going to calm down anytime soon. I run across the classroom to the big oak door. Running is also against the rules.

Mrs. Greames stands up from behind her desk and tries to hurry toward the door to block my way. The skin that hangs from her neck and arms sways back and forth in time with the clop-clop of her waddling steps. Some of the kids start laughing. She yells to me—even though yelling is against the rules—"Tracy, get back here this minute!"

I whirl around on one foot and glare at her. *"She's my fucking sister!"*

I scream this so loud and with so much fury that Mrs. Greames jumps back. The principal, Mr. Conway, hears and comes out of his office. He's bald and tall with a huge veiny nose. His shirt never buttons over the fattest part of his stomach.

"Miss Kachinsky! Stop!"

I try to sprint past him, but he grabs my arm with his kielbasa fingers. It hurts.

"Stop right there, young lady. The garbage that comes out of your mouth..."

I can still hear Jody sobbing, or I think I can. Now Mr. Conway's got me by both arms. He looks at me like I'm a rabid rat. I can't wrestle myself out of his grip. A rageful survival instinct takes me over at the exact moment I hear Jody howl again.

So I swing back my right leg, and I kick him square in the nuts.

I take off outside and find Jody, still crying on the rough black ground. There's sticky tar on the back of her dress and on her bare legs. Her white nylon ankle socks are stuck down into the backs of her scruffy saddle shoes. Her face is all blotchy pink. Her little blue plastic barrettes hang like Grandpop's fishing lures from the ends of her hair.

"C'mon," I say, and grab her hand. We run out the chain-link gate, down the hill, and around the back of the tannery.

I know my way around that leather yard, and I know Conway doesn't. I pull Jody down to duck behind a stinking stack of fresh blue hides. Jody's gasping, still sobbing, leaning on me. I'm shivering, sweating, scared.

We don't speak for a good five minutes. Our breathing slows as the panic finally begins to lessen. It appears that we have not been chased. Jody turns her head toward me, her eyes only inches from mine. Her puffy sad face looks like despair and terror in a tiny package. It's more painful to see that on my sister's face than it is to feel it myself. I look back at her steadily.

"I said *fuck* to Mrs. Greames."

Her eyes widen. "You're in trouble, Track."

"Yeah, I know."

"You're going to get the stick."

"Yup."

"And they're gonna call Mama."

"Prob'ly."

"Am I gonna get the stick?"

"No, you didn't do anything. I'll say I made you come with me."

"Track, what are we gonna do now?"

"Don't worry. I'll figure something out. Know what else?"

"What?"

"I kicked Conway in the nuts."

She gasps. "Did not."

"Did too."

Jody's shoulders start shaking even before she smiles. I snicker through my nose. Jody starts hee-hee-heeing. I watch pure awe transform those tired crying eyes. What a feeling.

Just then the twelve-fifteen factory whistle blows. It's a deep, deafening, familiar sound that fills our ears and drowns out our fear. It creates a kind of loud protective silence, a space for our own noise. We howl from our mouths, our throats, our lungs and hearts. We struggle to breathe; the laughter is suffocating. My mind is savoring the memory of Mr. Conway's eyeballs popping out and that soft thud as my foot made contact with his privates. I'm seeing Mrs. Greames's chicken neck waving like mad under her chin. I try to tell Jody this, but I can't get the words out.

The hysteria is depleting us. We can't sit up anymore, so we lay on our backs, stamp our feet, hold our bellies, and hoot like cartoon coyotes until I think I'm going to pee my pants.

And just for a sacred, precious moment when I am finally able to take a deep breath, I know some things I didn't know before. I know I can save my sister from the ferocious crying fits. I know I can zoom through purple puddles unscathed. I know that Mr. Conway will never be able to find me if I don't want him to. I know Grandpa will never really be dead. I know I can fly.

wide open song

When the rules for right conduct fall away,
and the power of external authority
drops away too,
I listen to the steady building
of my own voice
gaining momentum until it breaks free
into a wide open song.

It's me singing this melody
alive and kicking,
breaking free into the light,
swinging like a child again
all the way to China.

This is power that can never be taken away,
although there are names and places
that diminish the voice back to a whisper,
back underground
to begin the slow fight again,
the push for freedom
that can never be stifled.

poem for the woman who doesn't want a daughter

I want you to look at yourself in the mirror & say
"& God created Woman & she is good"

I want you to look at yourself in the mirror
& say "God is a Woman"

I want you to look at yourself in the mirror
& say "I am God's Daughter"

I want you to look at yourself
with a lover's eye
& write a poem about yourself that way

I want you to taste yourself & feel yourself & smell yourself
& study how to please yourself
the way you study
the way you were trained to study
to please men

I want you to study women walkin' down the street
the way you study men
How their hips swing & their breasts sway
& their hair goes free in the wind
& I want you to exult & sing
"I am one of them"

I want you to bathe yourself like a baby
with scented oil till you gleam

I want you to watch the muscles of women ripple
& say to yourself
how beautiful it is when women are strong

I want you to go to your hairdresser
& say "I want it natural
I like the way I am"

I want you to go through a hundred women's magazines
& tear out every page on cosmetics & beauty care
& how to reduce yourself to a shadow
& make a fire & let them burn

I want you to boycott perfumed toilet paper
& use an outhouse for a week
in the heat of the summer
& sit there with the door hangin' open
& look out at the trees

I want you to study proud women
& character lines
in the faces of old women
& think on every woman in your life
who did you good

I want you to find a portrait
of a great woman
& paste it over your television screen

I want you to ask for help from other women
& help them in return

& every time you feel turned on
I want you to close your eyes & say
"This is me
This comes from within"

a woman in perfect progress

My daughter refuses to pluck spreading
brow or anoint chapped lips and hands.
She rejects the bra that binds,
preferring to drape herself
in too-large T-shirts. Her tightly
tied braid grips knobby backbone,
while she chases the almighty
ball around polished courts.

Sweat collects in bursting
flower patterns on kelly green
cotton tanks. A new yet already grimy
knee brace begins to fray and zebra-
striped sneakers squeal in wild motion.
She rebounds, shoots, smiles from the floor.

She is fluid and fury,
stretching high to reject,
breaking free, sweeping
gravity reversed, breathless
intensity. She is tight,
toned, stronger than she knows.
She is a woman in perfect progress.

gypsy lore

"He comes in. He goes out. He comes in and he goes out. That's all," the gypsy said.

Anna listened and played with the topaz birthstone ring her parents had given her two years before, on her thirteenth birthday.

She'd first met the gypsy one July afternoon when she was shopping in midtown for a bikini, which she'd never bought, because they'd all been too low cut and she felt too flat chested. She'd grown hungry, and she saw a sign: "Gypsy Fortune Teller. Lunch and Supper served." Anna went upstairs. The room was dark and gloomy, and there were no other customers. The gypsy sat alone at a large table. Against the wall were some folding chairs.

Anna stood in the doorway and stared. The gypsy was bald in spots and had sparse yellow hair. She wore a cotton kerchief with a gaudy floral design, but it was falling off. She was haggard and heavily made up. Her earrings were black-plastic squares with red, shiny triangles hanging on the bottom.

"May I see a menu?" Anna asked.

"You want egg salad or tuna fish?" the gypsy replied. She sounded tired.

Last year, right before her fourteenth birthday, Anna had gotten food poisoning from bad mayonnaise. "Neither. Just my fortune." She hoped that the gypsy wasn't offended.

The gypsy told Anna's fortune with cards. "One day soon you'll go to Europe or maybe California. You'll go to a big entertaining, too."

"An entertaining?"

"A party. You'll go to a big party," the gypsy explained, as Anna handed her ten dollars.

Anna went back every week. She didn't believe a word that the gypsy said, but she went back anyway. Every Saturday morning she joined three old women there. None of them ever spoke to her. But the gypsy liked Anna and always took her last so that they could talk. "Annie," she would say, "you're a young girl. I only wish I were so young. Marry rich. Don't go for love. Just money."

On Saturday afternoons, Anna took an art course. She was frustrated. "You must learn to see," the instructor would frown. "Is that what the model looks like?" Anna looked at what she had drawn: The boy in the dream that she'd had the night before.

Anna had two real girlfriends. Anna liked Mindy best, but she was away, working as a counselor at a summer camp. Barbara, who was home, wore pigtails and cute dotted swiss blouses, and her voice was loud. Barbara had been seeing a boy steadily for the last two years. Barbara wasn't a virgin. "I've been doing it with Joe for a year, I guess," she'd told Anna. "You don't know what you're missing." But Anna wasn't envious of Barbara because Joe, Barbara's boyfriend, had bad breath.

Barbara got Anna a date with Peter, one of Joe's friends, although Anna hadn't asked her to.

They went out on a double date. Peter chain-smoked and had dirty fingernails. "Do you smoke?" he asked Anna.

"No." Silently she added, "I hate you. Go away."

They were in a movie theater. He put his hand on Anna's thigh. She had worn a new dress just in case he turned out to be cute. She removed his hand. A few minutes later he put it back, even higher. Barbara and Joe were kissing and Anna could hear Joe breathing. She could imagine how bad his breath was just from the sounds he made. The movie was about a mother of two who falls in love with her husband's psychiatrist. Anna felt that she understood the tormented actress with her frightened, sensual eyes. Peter left his hand on Anna's thigh for the rest of the movie. He didn't move his fingers up and down or rotate them along her stocking. His hand just remained there—menacing and greasy. After the movie, they went to an ice cream parlor that boasted waitresses in red leotards. Peter kept saying, "I'm gonna pinch one, I swear."

Barbara laughed. "Let's see."

Peter was eating a chocolate sundae. Some of it dripped on his chin.

Anna was sickened. "You have stuff on your chin."

Peter was embarrassed and wiped it off with Anna's napkin.

Anna told the gypsy about Peter. "He tried to unhook my bra later at Joe's house."

The fortuneteller shook her head. "Don't let him do that. Not him. He knows nothing. That's not the way."

One day, Anna bought the gypsy a gift: a box of chocolate-covered cherries. The gypsy kissed her cheek and laughed. "Annie," she said, "you are like these chocolates, so innocent." She and Anna finished the box of chocolates together. Finally, Anna said, "What's it like?"

The gypsy laughed very hard. "I'll tell you. He comes in and goes out. That's it."

Anna made her repeat it again. "Tell me more," she insisted.

"There's not much more. First it's some kissing. You know how to kiss already. That much you know. Then you touch each other. Then you touch each other some more. Then he comes in. That's it, Annie. The whole thing. There's not so much to it. That's why you should marry for money."

"Sometimes I dream that I'm doing it," Anna pleaded. "But I can't imagine what it feels like. Really feels like. Inside and all."

The gypsy shook her head. "Stop, Annie. You embarrass me. One day soon enough you'll see and then Big Deal. You'll see."

Anna went to the beach one Sunday with a girl that she knew slightly, whose parents were friends of Anna's parents. Karen went often and had a deep tan. Anna felt conspicuous in her whiteness. Two boys sauntered over. "Hi. You girls want company?" Karen made room for them on the blanket. The boys had a blaring radio with them. They placed it on the blanket and sat down. "Where are you girls from?"

"Deer Park." Karen crossed her legs. "You boys come here a lot?"

"Yeah. A lot." They were both very tanned. One was named Kevin and one was named Ronnie. Anna put on a big smile and told them about her art class. Kevin seemed bored, but Ronnie said, "I used to draw, too. Real wild things. My mother was scared of my drawings."

Anna thought maybe she liked Ronnie. He held her hand. Kevin announced that he and Karen were going for a walk. Ronnie and she listened to music until they came back. Karen was flushed, and she tried to mouth some words to Anna, but Anna couldn't understand. "Our turn to take a walk," Ronnie said. Anna rose and followed him, wishing she'd bought that bikini after all. Her modest two-piece bathing suit seemed dowdy.

She and Ronnie walked to a section of the beach that was rocky and deserted. He leaned over and kissed her. Her toes curled in the sand, and for the first time she thought maybe she was excited. She pressed herself against him and he pushed her down, awkwardly. He fell on top of her. He put his hand inside her bathing suit top. She rubbed his neck, because Barbara had once told her that Joe always got hard when she did that to him. Anna kept rubbing his neck. He put his hand on her stomach. She felt excited, but frightened, too. What if he put his hand in the bottom of her suit? What if he had a condom with him, and wanted to go further? She felt his hand sliding downward. Should she keep rubbing his neck? His hand was inside. She closed her eyes and tried to focus: She imagined that his hand was a foreign traveler with a French accent and that her body was an unfamiliar country. It made the roving fingers feel less like roving fingers. She wanted to be thrilled, to feel joyous, but she felt ticklish instead. "Stop," she said, softly, trying to sound sensual, not scared. His hand slowly emerged. He sat up, his face was sweating. Anna felt proud, and she kissed him lightly, just for an instant. She told him her phone number and they walked back to the blanket.

Anna and Karen went to the movies the next day.

"Do you like Kevin?" Anna asked Karen as the woman with the flash-light passed their row.

"I think so. He's a great kisser. And he's cute, especially with that little beard he's growing. Do you like Ronnie?"

"Yes." She paused. Karen seemed to expect more. "He's also a great kisser."

The next week, Peter, Anna's chain-smoking date, called. "No, I can't see you again," she told him. "I have a boyfriend now." Actually, Ronnie hadn't even called yet. And Kevin hadn't called Karen.

Anna missed the next Saturday at the art school and the gypsy's. Her mother's cousin had a family gathering in Woodmere and Anna's moth-er insisted that she come. Anna wore an outfit that her mother had picked out for her: blue leggings and an oversized sweater that was much too big and kept sliding off her shoulders. Her thirteen-year-old cousin, Bill, who wore braces, asked her to dance. She said she had a sprained ankle, and she sat with her parents. She drank too much of her father's red wine and felt sick. Her mother had to give her Alka-Seltzer when they got home.

The gypsy opened her door late the following Saturday morning. Anna and the three old women waited together on the staircase. Anna was silent, and the women talked among themselves. Finally, the gypsy appeared. She wore a paisley kerchief on her head, and a pair of green, swishing earrings that Anna had never seen before. The three women had their fortunes told. Anna heard the gypsy say to one of them, "Your son is fine. He hasn't written because he's been busy. You'll hear from him very soon. And he'll have good news for you."

Anna didn't listen any more until it was her turn. She had meant to buy the gypsy some more chocolate candy but had forgotten.

"So what happened last week, Annie? Because I have a great surprise for you." The gypsy spoke with more animation than usual. Her green earrings swished loudly. "My nephew just arrived from Hungary. He's eighteen. He's staying with me now, in my apartment downtown, and he'd like to make friends. I told him all about you. You don't have to date him. Just show him around the city a little bit." She took Anna into the back room, where she had never been before. It was half kitchen, half bedroom.

A good-looking boy sat on the bed. He was dark and had the beginnings of a mustache. His clothes weren't stylish but he looked romantic in his beige turtleneck and navy blazer. He greeted Anna with a smile and a thick accent. Anna sat down next to him on the bed. The gypsy sat on his other side. The three of them ate tuna fish sandwiches.

"You like it here?" Anna asked.

"So far." He smiled again.

"He's only been here a week, Annie," the gypsy said, standing. "Give him time to decide."

The boy laughed.

Anna wasn't sure how well he understood what was being said. "I have to go," the gypsy said. "I have customers."

Anna and the boy went for a walk. "Where do you and your aunt live?" She realized that she didn't know where the gypsy's apartment was.

"Twenty-third Street," he said. "The eastern part."

Without speaking, they walked toward the gypsy's apartment. Anna had already missed part of her art class and she felt guilty. Her mother would shout, "What am I paying good money for if you're going to take off whenever you feel like it?" But Anna didn't care: being with this boy was so much more exciting than standing in a drafty room in front of an easel.

As they crossed Third Avenue, Anna said, "You see that hot dog man? That's a New York specialty."

The boy glanced at the fat man and his hot dogs. He smiled vaguely, and Anna wondered again how much he understood of what she said to him.

He had a key to the gypsy's apartment. The apartment wasn't what she'd expected: no wild fabrics; no exotic music; no dancing sisters and uncles. The living room was bright and modern, with an orange sofa, a large TV, an Elvis clock, and a photograph of a young, blonde woman holding a plump baby in her arms. Anna turned away from the photo.

The boy went into the kitchen and came back sipping from a can of Pepsi. She walked toward him. "I'd like a sip." He understood immediately and handed her the can. She barely tasted it. She sat down on the sofa, delighting in the vibrancy she felt. The boy seemed to sense it, and sat down beside her.

Anna was conscious of her every move. She threw her arms around the boy's neck and kissed him. His tongue felt like a fuzzy peach. He began to pant. She rubbed his neck. He panted harder. Anna lay down. "No mind, just body," she whispered. The boy looked at her. "Nothing," she said. She got bored. She moved his hands all over her body but was dissatisfied. She sat up. "Listen. I'll sleep with you."

The boy's eyes were closed. "OK," he said, opening his eyes. Standing, he undressed quickly, not looking at her. He sat back down on the sofa.

Anna got undressed, feeling embarrassed, trying to appear graceful, although he was looking away. She left her clothes on the floor. She stared at him. He was thin and wiry. He met her gaze, then closed his eyes again.

She wasn't quite ready yet. She removed her topaz birthstone ring and placed it inside her pocketbook. Then she was ready, and she walked to the boy, wondering idly where the gypsy thought they were.

And then the boy was everywhere, all at once. She, too, closed her eyes. It hurt a little, but not for long. He seemed to know what to do, how to move, how to touch her breasts and her belly while he moved himself, faster and faster, inside her. It seemed like one of her dreams: imagined; vague; unreal.

He sat up. "I love you," he said. His voice was hoarse.

Anna stared at the ceiling. The gypsy had been right, after all: in and out and at last, finally over.

She felt tired, but invigorated, too. She'd learned a lesson today, in this boy's arms, a more important lesson than any she might have learned in art class. And the lesson was this: She would wait to make love again until she was ready, until she had grown up to be a powerful woman, not a girl any longer, a woman as powerful as the gypsy herself.

eve

The skin was scarlet and bitter
where her lips wrapped around it
and her teeth broke it open.
"Mpf," she said to the serpent
as she pulled the apple away from
her mouth. "Why'd He demand
we never eat this? It tastes foul."

"You're still thinking of surfaces,"
said the serpent. "The point is
you can learn anything
once you get past the skin.
Surely you're curious?"

"Anything such as what?"
asked Eve, peeling red
fragments, gulping before
their gall bit her tongue.

"Such as the truth about how
you were born," said the serpent.
"Discard that propaganda
about your arrival from Adam's
rib. That's merely another
in the series of men's displaced
womb-worshipping tales. Forget
the story about him being
an assemblage of mud, glued together
with God's spit, though that
has a splash of truth."

         "Mmm,"
said Eve, licking the golden
flesh beneath the skin.
"This tastes sweeter."

         "Bite it,"
said the serpent, "eat. You'll learn
what is right and wrong when you break
the rule. That will please Him.
You'll become the creature that He
loves best, the one that chooses,
the one that is free."

the dancing girl's story

You think you know what you've got here. Don't you think I can read your face? The set of your lips, the squint of your eyes. One of *those* women, you think. A bad woman. The kind who lies. You look at me and I know exactly what you're thinking: We've seen this kind of woman before. In the war. In the bars. In the hold of this ship.

I've seen them too, these women. I can recognize the signs, the same as you. They look tired.

But look at my face. No, look closer. Don't worry, I'm used to it. The stares. This face has worn well. I've had a thousand lovers, two thousand. Each has touched this face. A thousand years. You may not see. I do look young for my age. But I remember. Each year. Or more importantly, each man.

Don't worry. Sit down. I'll answer your questions. I'll tell you about myself. From the beginning, as you say.

When I was young, just born, risen from the sea, foam and salt still clinging to my ankles, my skin glistening wet, I danced smiling, eyes burning, I wanted to see everything at once, taste everything, I couldn't keep my mouth shut, I couldn't keep my eyes open wide enough. I danced barefoot on the sandstone, the scent of incense and sandalwood clinging to my breasts, the silk of my skirt smooth against my thighs. I danced watching everything at once. I was so young then.

I remember the first man, a minor court official, I've forgotten his name. He was nervous, he cast his eyes down, staring at the ground when I smiled at him. Later, when I touched the small of his back, the arch of his right foot, the curve of his left ear, he blushed. But then he did not look away. He looked into my face and said he loved me, would love me forever, as if he could. He was very young. I remember his cousin, a boy who danced so well I could feel the beat of his steps through the stones of the floor, through the soles of my bare feet. He made love like a dancer, touching my cheek. I felt the energy of his entire body in that one stroke. But perhaps it was not the cousin, but another man, a visitor from another nation far away. He came through the mountains on foot, carrying his tribute to Angkor in an embroidered bag, a nervous young man very far from home come to visit the palace. He stayed with us for three years. His skin tasted of the forest, pine and cedar. You see, history is wrong, a myth, if you believed I was confined to royalty. I was created to be pleased, not merely to please, though I can do that as well.

Where was I? My face. This face was meant to beguile. It's never been my intention to cause pain. But what can I do? I live forever and the men don't. I remember the Chinese magistrate. Such a funny man, he stayed for ten years, each was his last, then he would go home for good, he said. Then he was here twelve years, then twenty or more. He kept a journal. He showed me the neat columns of his beautiful script. Queer little pictures, I said. He recorded ten years of banquets, every fish he ever ate, the colors of the silks that the elephants wore for parades, the wild boar fights. And never once mentioned me. These catalogs of food and ceremony, he said, were for his emperor. It was important he record only matters of concern to the state, he said. Gudgeons and freshwater congers are matters of concern to the state, I said, but not dancing girls? I'll never understand the Chinese.

I don't hold grudges.

He had a wife and child at home, far away, all those years. His wife couldn't read or write, so he wrote to his brother to inquire about their health, and his brother always wrote that they were well and that they were pleased his post had brought so much honor to the family. Yes, stay, his brother wrote. And remember to write the governor, your cousin is studying for the official examinations and needs a tutor. See what you can do for us. Our father sends his blessings. Our mother sends her love. Your son is coming to resemble you, he is now five years old. Seven years old. Fifteen. So the Chinese man stayed with us. He was not needed at home.

He grew older as I stayed young. His belly round, his skin soft, loose under my fingers, his black hair grey then white, the lumpy shape of his skull exposed. I lay with him sweating and warm throughout the night, the sound of his heart racing, the firmness of his flesh, the prompt attention, so flattering, as later I lay with him cool cool throughout the night, the mosquito nets drawn tight against the bedroll to protect his soft flesh, his breathing labored, slow, as I put my palms against his forehead and kissed him good-bye. But all that was long long ago.

This face, the one you see before you, came later, with the war. No, I don't know which one. There've been too many. Do they all have names?

Let me tell you a secret. About living. About immortality. How does one live forever, I mean, really truly live? Have you ever imagined? The secret: I live like you. Each moment, each day, each year. We can only live in the present after all. Good or bad. Slow and dull as well as exciting and fun, so much fun. Otherwise, how absurd if we all left or intervened or flew away at any moment, whenever things started to drag. Why endure anything? Why not be a bird, a cloud, the wind? This is how I live, have lived. You understand?

But then I did leave, didn't I? After everything. I'd never done that before. It's hard to explain this feeling I had. But things had changed. It was time.

The rabid dogs came to the temple one night, circling the dusty footpaths, filling the air with snarls and spit. I heard their breath competing with the wind, heavy and wet, coming closer.

The men would come later, marching in stiff boots with leaden steps. They had shed their robes for uniforms of a dull brown, like olive pits, traded their smooth, wooden staffs for shiny guns.

I left before the men arrived. I stepped from the wall, hand to my diadem, careful not to let it catch in the stone as I walked onto the earth. You may think it cruel, I did not stop to tell my sisters good-bye. But they were sleeping, and I wanted to go.

I lit the joss sticks before the statue of Buddha and let the smoke caress my skin, fill the folds of my skirt. Sentimental perhaps. I pressed my hands together and touched the tips of my fingers to my forehead.

The wind called to me, pushed aside the vermilion streamers surrounding the altar. I felt them flick my shoulders, my calves, like a flame as it's snuffed between two fingers. I heard the dogs fighting, closer now, so close I could smell the blood on their fur. I gathered up my carp, poor thing, neglected in the stone bowl by the door, and ran on tiptoe to the temple entrance. I slipped my feet into the straw sandals by the door; you see I wasn't thinking clearly. Why would I need shoes? I turned back once, bowed, then stepped out into the night. The wind carried me away.

My carp thrashed against my side, his sharp scales digging into my flesh. I pulled him closer, but he only wiggled more, afraid no doubt of this sudden plunge into the dark sky, so cold and dry. I remember when the fish were plentiful: black carp and tenches splashed in the rice paddies, jumped into nets.

I remember the monks on their visits were fascinated with my fish, played games with him, composing their impossible poems: "How do you catch the slippery carp? Pour oil on it. How do you catch the golden carp? With half a gourd." My carp, white and red with a black cap, tolerated them, surfacing for the crumbs they tossed into the pond, snapping his lips. They thought he was talking to them. "How many monks does it take to feed a fish?" we used to ask, giggling within earshot. "The answer? Ten. One to throw the crumbs and nine to write a poem about it."

To think, only my fish was left.

I flew above the banyan trees. The roots dangling from the branches clawed the air, reaching for my skirts. My poor fish shook, his body starving for water. His tail lashed against my back and I felt warmth rush from the wound, run down my sides. The fish wriggled less violently, my blood pouring over his scales, his thirst slaked.

I left the men and dogs behind to fight, their fur and hair, howls and shouts, swirling in the air. There was no room for me in a world where men mixed with dogs. Can you understand?

How long did I travel? Years. Lifetimes. It's all the same.

Endlessly I searched the horizon for the glimmer of a wave. To the west I saw the purple mountains, spotted with fire. To the south, the edge of the forest crept toward the sand. But it was the desert, not the beach. Meteorites like lightning bolts streaked across the sky but the moon hid her face.

Below, the little people fled in the night on foot, generations walking toe to heel, toe to heel, in lines like thin snakes across the countryside. I followed one woman holding a baby that would die three miles later from its fever and a little girl who would survive a year and a young boy who was very thirsty and ran a step away from his mother between the bodies toward a pool of water which only he with his bright child's eyes had seen reflecting the stars. He stepped lightly and the click like a bone against a bone froze everyone in the line exactly as they were, toe to heel, frozen in each other's footsteps. "Don't move," the old woman in front cried. "Don't move." The mother looked at her son, felt the weight of the hot baby burning her arm. The young boy wanted to cry. He looked to his mother. The line began to move on, wearily but with purpose. "Don't move," the old woman in front called to the boy. Toe to heel, toe to heel the families moved forward until the mother was left facing her son who had begun to cry. She wanted to join him, despite the baby and the little girl. Her lips moved, "Don't move don't move don't move." She will whisper this forever. And in that moment as the wind picked up, she looked up into the cool breeze into my face. I smiled at her, my face beguiling. She forgot to whisper and the boy moved. The instant before his head was blown from his body thirteen feet behind his mother, I reached out and snatched his soul and held it in the palm of my hand. The wind was warm from the explosion and we were pushed forward far away from his mother who stared after me, her mouth filled with her voice, and I left the line of little people far behind. We raced above the clouds into the light of the moon. And I tossed the boy into the sky where the wind grabbed hold of him and rushed away. I'm not supposed to intervene. It's true. The cycles of birth and rebirth. But you were not in my position.

My wings grew, beating the air, my hair streaming behind me like the tail of a kite. My skirt fell off into the wind and my legs were freed, to kick and bounce against the air. The mouth of my fish pressed against my ribs, opening, closing.

At last the scent of the ocean tickled my nostrils. I fell, my wings glistening in the light of the rising sun, sparkling with the white salt embedded in the traces of my blood. My arms grew tired, I drew them closer to my body, my legs grew close. My fish leapt from my side, plunging into the smooth water with a wag of its tail. Like a dragon I dove in beside him, the cool water slipping across my body. I rolled against the soft waves like fine silk. I slept.

Until you found me.

Caught in that net with the ugly, mute fish that are glassy-eyed and smelling like decay. The fishermen pulled me to the surface and dropped me on the deck of their boat. Then your men came, in their white soldiers' clothes, pulled me by the arms from the thrashing bodies, and pushed me into the dark room packed with the thin dark people, the still children and the silent babies. Then you, it was you, not I, remember, who asked me to come into your room and answer your questions. And all the while you sit there, you and the other man with the tape recorder and the dictionary and the pile of papers, you take notes and I talk and you ask me more questions.

And now you look at me like that.

I am not crazy. I will not be dismissed, so you'd better sit back down. Sit.

You with your questions. Do-I-fear-for-my-life-do-I-fear-political-reprisal-why-have-I-come-to-*this*-country? Why-didn't-I-stay-where-I-came-from-do-I-have-family-here-do-I-think-I-can-make-money? "I—N—S?" you say slowly, enunciating each letter. "Do you understand?" Do I?

I am not crazy. And I am not a liar.

You wanted me to tell you everything. Everything, you said. I've told you.

But can *you* understand? That's my question.

black woman

i'm adaptable:
i bend
i fold
i integrate perception
i walk
a million miles
in a canyon's
depth of fire
i'm mistrusted
& ignored
thru a spectrum
of emotion
my pleas for
understanding
nurture streams
of nonsupport
i march
to hidden rhythm
in the aftermath
of justice
unveiled against
the grain
i adjust
to cool surroundings

at the gym i go to

At the gym I go to you wouldn't feel out of place. Who could? We get beefy twentysomething guys but we also get their grandmas. We get dancers. We get fat people who walk on the treadmill. We get stroke patients—one man drags his leg as he moves from machine to machine and his nurse cheerfully tells him to suck it up and get a move on.

There's nothing like a little blood pumping through the veins—and it'd be a lot cheaper than your shrink, who seems to be doing a lot more siphoning than pumping, anyway. Looking in the mirror and watching a muscle move is a fine thing. And here's what I've found out: The heart is just another muscle. It can get strong too; like it works out with your biceps; it can keep your quads company.

I'll tell you a story; maybe it'll help:

I started going to the gym to watch someone. I'd put my makeup on and shine my sneakers and then he would pick me up and we'd head to the gym so I could watch him play basketball. I'd sit in the bleachers with a row of other watchers; we watched our men—our fortunes rising and falling with their shooting fate—and we talked about our men's cars and we admired one another's hair and we traded notes about our sneakers. And the whole time, I'd think:

When did the aliens show up in their spaceship and take over my body?

Go ahead and laugh. I deserve it. I can take it. But after you spend all day in an office without windows, listening to the drone of middle-aged men's projections and objections, you do crazy things. Like turn yourself into a bimbo. Comic relief, but I wasn't laughing.

His name was Frank and he went to my high school. He had biceps bigger than my thighs and he had a chip in his front tooth that made him look dangerous. And dangerous thawed me. If you're as bad off as I was you know what I mean when I say that I'd have taken resuscitation anyway I could get it. A muscle-bound car salesman wasn't such a bad deal.

He sold me my Geo. Here's the scene:

The woman leans over, looking anxiously at the window sticker which bears no resemblance to the page in the car-buyer's guide.

"You look like someone who knows what she wants," he says to the woman.

She laughs. She looks at the smooth face, the slicked hair, the spread of shoulders. And thinks: OK, I'll buy. The car. You. Whatever.

He leans on a baby blue sedan and points a finger at her.

"I see you in red," he says. "Very sexy."

She fights the sarcasm worming its way from head to mouth. She plugs the words but can't quite dismiss the sneer.

"No, not red," he says, reading her mouth. "Jade. You're definitely jade."

"I am?"

You take it from there. One day I'm a desperately depressed woman feeling the squeeze of years and my ballooning body—and I trade it in for the squeeze of tight jeans and an arm around me. I diet. I go on birth control pills. I start smoking on the sly. I drink every night. I cut work on his days off when he tells me to. I sit and watch him play basketball three nights a week. He pounds the boards and then struts off the court. I fall asleep in a meeting at work, drool on my copy of the contract, and the old men are so embarrassed that it's hard to remember who the idiot is.

So here's the next scene:

The game ends. While she's waiting for her guy to finish up his postgame ritual, she watches another guy strut off the court, his basketball trapped between his arm and body. A kid behind him shoots wildly at the hoop and the boy's ball knocks the guy in the head.

He curses at the kid and throws the kid's ball out the open door of the gym.

She's still watching. She looks at the women beside her. They are looking at their sneakers. None of them will claim this guy. She looks at the men walking off the court beside the man; they are laughing. The kid has run out to find his ball.

"You bully," she says.

The men look up at her. Then they laugh. She is making a joke, they've decided.

Her man smiles nervously, his broken front tooth makes his smile look crooked.

"Let's go," he says to the woman.

She climbs down the bleachers, her tight jeans and her little sneakers make the climbing slow and jerky. She is flushed when she reaches the gym floor.

The man with the chipped tooth puts a hand on her arm and squeezes a little too hard. This is his way of telling her to behave, of reminding her who is in charge, of declaring who all of this is about.

Out of the corner of her eye she sees the boy come through the door, back into the gym. She ignores the pressure on her arm and she looks over to where the boy pretends to be busy with his shoe, biding his time until the men have left the gym.

"Give me the ball," she says to the man.

She has to say it louder before he gives it to her.

She walks across the gym to the basket near the boy and throws the ball up at the basket. The boy jumps to his feet, as though she has called him by name. He dribbles on the court and arcs a shot over the woman's head. She throws the ball at the hoop for several minutes before, by some miracle, one of her shots bangs its way through the hoop. Only then does she leave with the man who has been waiting and watching.

I have a point. I'll get to it. Or maybe I won't. But I'll tell you: that was it for Frank. One transgression and I didn't get another chance. I was too marginal to begin with. But I went back. I wore sweatpants and I took myself on a night I knew Frank didn't play. In between the pickup games I heaved the ball up at the basket with the kids and the old guys.

The third time I went back, this big guy came over to me. "May I?" he asked me and reached for the ball. "Watch." He shot the ball in slow motion so I could see everything he did. Then he brought the ball back and helped me shoot. I'd always tried to muscle the ball through the hoop, heaving as hard as I could, but the power doesn't come from the muscles of your arms. Did you know that? It comes from the flick of your wrist. You have to wave at the basket as you push the ball up. That's what he showed me. Physics. Touch.

Then I noticed the weight room. I'd walked past it every time I went to the gym to watch Frank play, but it had never registered.

It doesn't take long to get over the feeling you don't belong. You watch people the first few times. You get an idea of the physics of the place. And then you're at home there.

So here's the next scene:

She's at work. She tears the wrapping paper off and opens the box. She pulls out a sweatshirt and a pair of sweatpants. A card flutters to the ground. One of the old guys picks it up and hands it to her. "We'll miss you, Champ," it says.

And she wants to tell them what she's learned: Don't be afraid. Age, money, bosses, loneliness—they're just a squeeze on your arm. They're bullies.

"Thanks," is what she says.

And she pulls on her sweatshirt and eats cake with the old guys. She is going to an office with less money and more windows. She will miss the old guys; that comes as a surprise. They cut her a second piece of cake.

Now you tell me that you can't this, can't that, can't anything since he left you.

And I say: You were dead before he left. This is what you have to do: Move. Get it? Move. Run, walk around the block, tai kwon do, tap, bike, bench press. Move.

The heart is just another muscle.

grit

I chew concrete, grit between my teeth
forever, since birth, didn't even notice.
It was in the milk, the potatoes,
the prayers and first grade lessons.
I liked it, didn't have to learn, didn't
know a meal or a day without it.
And the more concrete I ate,
the more it settled—in my feet,
took away a freedom never known,
no reason or thought to fight for it,
nor even to run away. I did not need
shackles. I did not need prison bars
to hold me in, being fed concrete
since day one, being told
all I couldn't and wouldn't
and shouldn't do.

I strain my food now, strain away
the grit, and take a smuggled chisel
to my feet each night, working
my way down to flesh and bone,
digging a tunnel to an angry voice
locked up tight in my toes, toes that
have never touched mud or music,
toes that ache every morning to laugh,
to run, to wiggle way up in the air.

illegal

At least a hundred women
wait patiently in line while
across the hall a door marked
"Men" stands empty. I watch
them flow quickly through—biology
allowing them to stand tall
while we undress and balance.

As curtain time draws near,
(pressed with the obvious)
I cross the hall, risk shock
instead of suffer through
this mounting pressure.
Soon others (who it seems
only needed someone to suggest
they could defect) begin
to run toward relief.

Our high heels click tick
in unison on marble floor,
and all I see (or care to see)
are heads, aghast and peering
over black suit, blue suit, brown suit
along the gilded urinal wall.

Amidst their disbelief, we fill
the empty stalls. And to think
we could have been arrested for being
in such urgent need, and
for hearing such a trickle.

common waters

I was sure I'd hit a rock and sink to the bottom of the Colorado River if I rowed a dory through the Grand Canyon. I'd already worked four summers rowing baggage rafts and flipping pancakes for free, just so I could be there. But in those early years, I didn't want to be a river guide, especially for the company I worked for. They rowed little wooden dories. I watched as they hit rocks and even sometimes turned the sixteen-foot boats upside down, people and oars floating everywhere. I was safe in the kitchen. While they patched boats in the evenings, I watched the charcoal and prepared the Dutch ovens of lasagne. I think I was about to cook my twenty-fifth trip when I was asked to row. A boatman had canceled at the last minute. Would I take the dory and hand over my pancake flipper to someone else?

My first dory was bigger than most—eighteen-foot, aluminum, and candy-apple red. She was a seasoned boat, pockmarked with the dents of summers long before my time. She wore the name Ootsa in cracked and peeling letters on either side of the bow. Her decks were painted dull grey, and I'd been told her hatches leaked and would need to be bailed out halfway through a big white-water day. The gunwales of the Ootsa were bruised and chipped, but somehow they met true at stern and bow. I felt a dim sense of security knowing the Ootsa had been down the Colorado more times than I. She might know her way around the rocks and waves somehow. As I slid the twelve-foot ash oars into her oarlocks, I looked around at my fellow crew members. We were lined up at Lee's Ferry, the starting point of our trip, fiddling with our boats, awaiting the passengers who would ride with us for twenty-one days.

Gunner was the trip leader. I had cooked for years Gunner's trips. I watched him navigate the rapids of the Colorado many times. We drank more than a few dark beers, admiring sunsets from the deck of his dory, the Phantom. I met him ten years ago in Idaho, when he was big and had friendly blue eyes and a full head of blond curly hair. Although I grew up in Idaho, I had never seen the rivers until I floated them in Gunner's boat. He showed me the Snake and Salmon Rivers, took me hiking, explained the geology. But most of all he told me about the water, how the currents moved and how a boat moved within them. When I was a kid, he invited me into his outdoor world and embraced my desire to learn.

Now that I was ready to row a boat through the Grand Canyon, Gunner seemed smaller, his frame slumped over slightly, frozen in the rowing position. He wasn't as inviting anymore, as if his skin had been hardened by years of exposure. On our last trip he was distant, like the far-off rims of the Canyon. He often stared at the river, watching the waters move, learning their secrets, but never sharing them anymore. He wore a hat all the time these days to hide his balding head, but his body was still solid and efficient. I figured he would support me even if I sunk the Ootsa.

I was the only woman on a crew of six. The aluminum Ootsa looked like a battered sardine tin compared to the five streamlined wooden dories lined up beside her. I watched as the guys loaded their boats with tents and beer and sleeping pads. I opened my own hatches again and looked at the spread of potatoes, onions, and basketball-size cantaloupe. Gunner said I was to carry all the fruit and vegetables for the twenty-one-day trip. He said I had to take care of them like they were my own floating garden. I knew the routine from cooking for so many years. I also knew that the produce boat was the heaviest boat of the trip for at least the first week.

Finally the bus with our passengers arrived. They got out, leaning over with the weight of their day packs, and stood gawking at us in the September morning sun. I gawked back, trying to anticipate who would ride with me. I must have looked odd to them, the only girl with the largest boat. What would they think? Hopefully they would assume I was very experienced and could handle the Ootsa like a precision sports car. I looked back at the dory, and her red sides seemed to expand and sigh as if she realized she had to do the trip one more time. A family of four ambled my way. I had no intention of telling them I had never rowed a dory in the Grand Canyon. I calculated their weights as they approached—about seven hundred pounds of passengers. Could I move that heavy a load down the river? I showed them where to stow their day packs and we were off, following Gunner down the Colorado.

There was no doubt about it, the Ootsa was heavy. I pushed on the oars, encouraging her lumbering bulk downstream. It wasn't long before all the guys were ahead of me. I expected that, however, and made a point of at least keeping them in sight. I knew we would pull to shore at Badger, the first big rapid, and scout the run. They would wait for me there. The family of four lounged against the sides of the boat with their feet up on the decks. The long stretch of calm water had built up their confidence. They asked me about myself—how long had I been rowing, where did I go to school, what made me want to run rivers? I mouthed answers to their questions, but my mind was on Badger and on how my reclining passengers would respond in heavy white water.

As we drifted around the final bend above Badger, I rowed toward the left bank and tied the Ootsa alongside the wooden dories. The width of her decks dwarfed the smaller wooden boats, making them look like toys. I hustled up to my fellow guides, anxious to hear what they thought about the run. The water was a little low, and I knew Badger was tricky for a dory at low water. As I approached the guys, Gunner was making wild gestures with his hands. His voice had a ring of panic to it, like a high school teacher loosing control of his class.

"It's that rock at the bottom of the tongue you gotta watch out for today. That'll take the bottom right off a dory."

I knew what rock he was talking about; I'd seen it do just that to more than one dory. I thought about the Ootsa's aluminum bottom. If I hit the rock it would dent the boat and sound a ring that would be heard up on the canyon's rim, but I'd probably get by without sinking, this time. Actually, I felt pretty good about the run. I knew if I pulled hard enough at the top, I could miss that rock altogether.

"Don't you think if you enter a little left it will set you up to miss that rock?" I asked Gunner.

"Look, if you don't know the run, you shouldn't even be here. You've got to know what you're doing to row one of these boats," Gunner said and walked toward his dory.

I stood there feeling like I'd been hit with a big stick. I did know the run, and I did know how to row, and he knew that. But he hadn't answered like the friend I'd known for ten years. I walked back toward the Ootsa trying to think only about getting through Badger.

I was fourteen when I met Gunner. His real name was Henry Ruckak, but everyone said he earned the name Gunner after pulling off some incredible run through Gunbarrel Rapid on the Salmon River long ago. He was a longtime dory boatman at the river company in Idaho. I was a kid working as warehouse help. It was a seasonal job for both of us and Gunner showed up every spring for the first trip of the season. Some of the boatmen were hippies who arrived in Volkswagen buses and walked barefoot on the cement floors of the warehouse. I noticed Gunner, however, always wore hiking boots with clean matching socks and symmetrical laces. He noticed me too, and even gave me a ride home one day in his black Ford van with Colorado plates. A calendar hung from the van wall and a plywood bed took up one corner. Gunner's Hawaiian shirts hung from a wire fitted across the back. As I got out of his van and approached the steps of my parents' house, I wondered what it would be like to live like Gunner.

When I started the job in the warehouse, I had no idea what a dory was, or even that there were flowing rivers in Idaho. Lewiston sat at the confluence of the Snake and Clearwater Rivers, but both resembled large, unmoving lakes at that point. I washed so many vehicles and did so many dishes that in August my boss let me go on a five-day Salmon River trip. Gunner was the trip leader and he told me it was my job to show the passengers how to paddle the Tahiti, a little two-person inflatable. I wasn't sure I knew how to paddle it, but I was thrilled with the responsibility Gunner placed on me, and I acted like I had been paddling all my life.

There were several teenagers on that trip, and we spent almost every day in the inflatables. Although Gunner had put me in charge, I managed to turn my inflatable over in three rapids. Each time, he laughed and pulled me out of the water onto the deck of his dory. He would catch my inverted inflatable, turn it over, and put me back in it with words of encouragement for the next rapid.

"You're a real Tahiti Kid," he would say. "Get back in that boat and paddle hard through the next rapid!"

I never let him know I was scared to death. I wanted him to think I was good and confident—a real white-water chick. I wanted him to think I'd be worth taking down the river again next summer.

The one day I gave up my inflatable on that five-day trip, I sat in the back of Gunner's boat watching the way he maneuvered through the rapids. I sat there all day watching his muscles move as he pulled and pushed on the oars, thinking about how he had called me the Tahiti Kid.

Gunner stood up on the deck of the Phantom for a final look as he drifted into Badger Rapid. I was two boats behind him, drifting in the current, waiting my turn. Once Gunner entered the rapid, he dipped out of sight. I waited for the telltale thud of wood hitting rock, but didn't hear anything. If I hit in the aluminum Ootsa, the entire canyon would know. If I tore the bottom of the Ootsa open, I knew Gunner would be there to pull me to shore and help fix it. He would slap me on the shoulder and say it happens to everyone—or would he? Would he share my mistakes as if they were common waters—something we all experienced, or would I have to keep them to myself, underwater, as if I'd done something wrong? Gunner's response to me at the scout must have been anxiety. He was, after all, rowing a wooden boat in fairly low water. And I wasn't. We would share a beer at camp and his words would be forgotten.

The Ootsa slid into the tongue of the rapid. Her weight gave her a mind of her own, and I was sure if I didn't line her up at the top, I would have no chance of changing her position in the rapid. I pulled hard on the oars, coaxing her toward the left. Reluctantly, she obeyed and we moved through the waves at the top, missing the rock at the bottom by two feet. My passengers cheered as they bailed water out of the Ootsa. I looked up, hoping to give Gunner the thumbs-up sign, but he was already a mile downstream, eyes focused on the flat water ahead. He hadn't seen my run.

Idaho winters are cold and cloudy, and I spent many of them in high school classrooms, looking out the window, remembering images from past summers, the people and rivers I had come to know. After that first river trip, I went on one or two every summer. Gunner was on all of them. Sometimes I was the Tahiti Kid, but more and more often he let me ride in the training raft and try the oars at easier rapids. I was still scared. The water didn't scare me; it was what I might do to the boat. And what Gunner would think if I wrecked. I wanted to fulfill all of his expectations. I wanted to learn to maneuver a boat like he did.

The memory that surfaced most often while sitting in math class was the one in which Gunner let me row his dory on the Snake River. I had been sitting behind him as usual, watching how he kept the boat in the current, feathering the oars with every stroke. Gunner stood up, let go of the oars, and stretched his arms high over his head.

"Why don't you take her for a while," he said.

The butterflies let loose in my stomach like they had just been freed from a long winter's sleep. My arms felt shaky and light as I moved into Gunner's rowing seat. The oars were heavy in my hands. I looked down-river trying to see every obstacle that might cause a problem. Gunner took a seat behind me and put a hand on my shoulder.

"Just relax and pretend you're the Tahiti Kid again," he said.

I took a few deep breaths and relaxed a little when I remembered this stretch of the river was all calm water. A sense of pride crept into my mind as I thought about what I was doing. I was rowing Gunner's dory.

Ahead, I saw water rising in little white splashes. My stomach clenched in fear, cramping like a vise grip. It looked like a rapid ahead, but I didn't remember it being there. I tried not to show my nervousness, and I figured Gunner would take the oars back soon anyway. I waited for him to get up and switch places. He didn't move. We got closer to the rapid, and finally I cast an anxious look in his direction.

"You got it," he said. "Just remember to pull away from the left wall at the bottom."

I tried to remember what the left wall looked like. I imagined it being this huge slab of black granite extending out into the river, waiting to smash Gunner's little wooden boat. I tensed as we dipped into the top waves. I realize now the waves were not big at all, but back then, they could have been ten feet tall. The dory sliced through the waves and then I turned it, preparing to pull away from the wall I still could not see. I heard Gunner in the back seat whooping and cheering like I'd just made it through Lava Falls on the Colorado. The water smoothed out again, and I turned the dory downstream. Gunner tugged on my life jacket.

"Great job," he said.

On the fourth night we always try to camp at Nankoweap. The Colorado River makes a big bend as it weaves around the delta of Nankoweap Canyon. At the far end is a beach partially sheltered by old mesquite and acacia trees. It's my favorite camp and as I rowed within sight of the beach, I was relieved to see it was empty and would be ours for the night.

After unloading the boats, I sat on the deck of the Ootsa and popped open a beer. Most of the dory boatmen considered the forty-five min-

utes after unloading gear personal time. This is the time when river stories are created, as boatmen remember and glorify the big wave that
nearly turned the boat over. I lay back in the front seat of the Ootsa and
sipped my beer. The dory's large grey seat cradled me like a baby in a
stroller. Kevin and Mark got off their dories and joined me, raising their
beers in a toast.

"Here's to you," they said. "You handle the Ootsa like she were a mere
bathtub toy."

"I don't know about that," I laughed. "She's more like a submarine, but
we get along."

I shifted my position in the Ootsa so I could see our camp. Several passengers sat in the sand, playing cards and laughing. Gunner had taken his
wooden chair down to the wet sand by the river. He was hunched over,
writing in his journal, toes digging into the sand as if anchoring himself
to the beach. He glanced up and caught my eye, but quickly looked
away. I stared at him for several minutes wondering why he didn't have a
beer on the Ootsa and share the day, the rapids, the water.

"Gunner, come on over. I got a cold one for you," I said.

"You know, I'm going to finish this paragraph and get to work," he said,
digging his toes deeper into the wet sand. "But thanks."

The summer after I graduated from high school in Idaho was the year I
first floated the Grand Canyon. I was on the trip as an assistant cook,
and Gunner was leading. Gunner told me my job was to help the cook,
ride in the training raft and bail, and do whatever I could to help
around camp. On that trip, I watched Gunner lead the boats through
some of the biggest white water I had ever seen. He negotiated waves,
fixed boats, and educated passengers like a true professional. I worked
harder on that trip than I had ever worked in my life. I looked at every
bend in that majestic river like I would never see it again. I tried to

imprint images of the two-hundred-and-eighty-mile journey in my mind, in case it was my last trip. After eighteen days of bailing, cooking, and hiking, I was asked to work the entire summer as a cook. And then I was asked back year after year.

When I was twenty-two, I moved to Flagstaff so I could be closer to the Grand Canyon. I rented an apartment and worked on a teaching certificate in the winter. I still thought anxiously about summers and my seasonal friends. One spring Gunner came into town for an early April trip. Since I was settled in Flagstaff, my place had become a landing pad for stray boatmen awaiting trips, and Gunner always stayed on the floor of the living room. We went out to dinner that night and I told Gunner about the two trips I had cooked without him.

"You should have been there last week when I burned the enchiladas, burned them bad," I said. "I needed you there to convince everyone of how good it still was!"

"That happens to the best cooks," Gunner laughed. "Besides, I hear you're rowing a raft these days too. When you do both, something is bound to go wrong."

"Maybe," I said. Gunner had always been supportive of me, but his comment seemed sour. "But I make it work fine."

"Yeah," he said. "I'm sure you do."

Late that April night I heard the door to my room open. I knew exactly what was going to happen. I guess I expected it. When Gunner climbed in beside me and took off my T-shirt, it seemed OK. I trusted him. Why shouldn't the closeness of all the years lead to this? As he made love to me, I slid my fingers into his thinning blonde hair and thought of the way the river slides against the shore. He stayed in my bed all night, but when I tried to snuggle against him, he tucked his arms around his pillow, turned his back to me, and stayed that way.

We approached Lava Falls on day eighteen. The Ootsa and I had made it through all the big white water so far. Her load of produce had diminished and her large red sides no longer expanded and sighed before me. She seemed resigned to finishing one more trip, but I knew Lava was another thing altogether. The crew hiked up a basalt-strewn slope and gathered on a shelf overhanging the river to look at Lava Falls.

"This is bad water for Lava," Gunner said, arms pointing toward the slot run like a general pointing out the enemy. "We've got to do the slot run, even though the water is a little high for it. You got to be right on it."

I looked at Gunner in his faded yellow baseball cap with the oversized bill. I remembered a trip in Idaho when he had let me wear that hat because I'd lost mine. I thought how I'd rather have the sun bake a hole in my head now, before I'd ask him for anything. I also thought about how I couldn't expect his support at Lava. I was on my own. It was like I had taken the river from him and he was holding on to what he had left, keeping it to himself. If I missed the run and flipped over, it might be my last dory trip through Grand Canyon. Gunner might say I was incompetent, that I shouldn't have been given a dory in the first place. I thought about how we hadn't sat together on the deck of the boats once this trip. I reached my hand up toward his shoulder. I could tell him I was sorry right now, before Lava. I was sorry for asking questions, sorry for rowing a dory down the river, just like he did. I'd even blow the run if it would make him feel better. I would jump out of my boat in the first wave, into the cold water. I'd let my boat crash into the rocks if it would make things like it used to be with Gunner. But I stopped my hand before it got to his shoulder.

I didn't ask any questions about the run. I was afraid of showing my fear. Although I'd never rowed the slot run, I'd seen it done and I used those memories as my guides. I clipped and unclipped my life jacket as Gunner discussed the order we would run.

"I want two groups of three. I'll go, then Mark, then you," he said looking at me. "Once we're through, then Bob, Randy, and Kevin. We need to stay close so we can run safety for each other."

The butterflies I'd felt rowing Gunner's boat in Idaho didn't compare to what I felt as I approached the Ootsa. It was more like a hungry pack of vultures had been turned loose to feed upon the contents of my stomach. My four passengers sat at attention, their eyes searching my face for some indication of what lay ahead.

"Lean into these waves and hang on tight," I said as I rowed out into the current behind Mark and Gunner, searching for the slot. The boatmen always said you can't really see the slot from above; you just have to believe it's there. I thought about this as I watched the water boil and froth, looking for my line. I remember watching Gunner drop in, but then my attention was entirely on the water. I kept the Ootsa at a slight angle until I was sure I was just above the slot. I straightened her up a little late, and hit the first big wave slightly sideways.

"High side," I yelled as my passengers leaned their weight into the wave, trying to counterbalance the dory. The wave blasted over the side of the boat, burying us all in water, and knocking the right oar out of my hand. Once the water drained from my eyes, I grabbed the oar back just in time to straighten out for the final three waves. As we crested over the last one I whooped in relief, only to be cut short by the sight of Gunner's upside-down dory floating just ahead.

Gunner was crawling up on the bottom of the capsized boat as I approached. I counted the bobbing orange jackets in the water. All of his passengers were there, but they were having trouble getting up on the slippery bottom of the boat. They couldn't help him right the boat unless they got on the bottom with him. Gunner looked downstream, the veins in his neck swelling like blistered skin.

"Get on the boat," he yelled at his swimmers. "We're about to hit another rapid."

I knew what rapids did to upside-down dories. "Take the oars and keep us as close as possible," I said to one of my passengers.

I knew it was risky to leave my boat, but I jumped into the river and swam over to help Gunner. He gave me a hand up on the glistening black bottom. We grabbed the flip fines and pulled the boat upright. I had just enough time to jump back on board the Ootsa and guide her through the next rapid. We regrouped at the first beach and popped a few bottles of champagne.

"That wave came from nowhere," I heard Gunner saying. "Nobody could have kept her upright in that situation."

"I looked back and you were gone," one of Gunner's passengers said. "And then I was swimming next to the upside-down boat."

"That's part of the program at times. You never know when the river will call for you," Gunner said.

Apparently he had been a little left of the slot and had turned over in the top wave. I knew my run had not been perfect either, and I could have flipped just as easily. I wondered what Gunner thought about me helping him. Someone handed him a dark imported beer and he was making big swooping patterns with the bottle as he relived his flip. I wanted him to talk to me and tell me thanks, or even tell me I should never have left my boat. I was hoping he might notice something, maybe that I was just as capable as him, and perhaps we could be friends again. Finally, I walked up to Gunner and put my hand on his shoulder.

"Pretty exciting back there, huh!" I said.

"Yeah. Good thing I went first so you could go to school and figure out where to go."

I took my hand off his shoulder and walked away.

Eventually, the Ootsa was retired. She now sits in the warehouse, on a shelf, watching over those who come and go. I think she probably knows the boatmen and women better than we know each other. She has taken us all down the river and knows our individual hopes and fears. We communicate with our boats in ways we cannot communicate with each other.

woman's work

Traveling through time
backward one thousand years
where Chumash Indian women
walked the same path as I
along the Arroyo Creek
in the Conejo Valley,
sheltered by giant oaks,
like ancient sages,
I come upon a sandstone boulder
with five bowl-shaped indentations
used as mortar to grind acorns.
My hand feels the gentle curvatures,
centuries of domestic toil.

My bones feel the pestle push and pull
of hundreds of women—
the aching labor of making acorn flour.
Three days work of five women grinding,
who then pour twenty baskets of water
to leach the bitter tannins
from powder placed upon sycamore leaves,
pure water filters through
leaving acorn meal white and sweet.

I see a Chumash woman weaving
a burden basket from green willow
which is strapped upon her torso,
like a womb preserving life,
for the collection of acorns.

I want to introduce myself
but realize they can't see me,
yet somehow after all these years,
we speak the same language,
feel the same aches—
accepting nature's way.

Umbilical cords connect our generations,
amniotic waters continue
to filter impurities.
Holy work of a woman
sustaining life's sweetness.

new politics in salem

LAURIE CABOT, A WITCH FOR ALMOST
40 YEARS, HAS ENTERED THE MAYOR'S
RACE IN SALEM, MASSACHUSETTS
(ASSOCIATED PRESS)

She always dresses in basic black
and provides her own transportation.
When she appears before an audience
she drives her opponent batty:
he squeals like a frightened pig.
Though men find her enchanting
the women are not jealous—
she's promised a handsome lover
in every woman's bed.
She offers to bring in new industry:
a bottling plant for the potions,
a newt ranch, the guano works,
a boom in copper pots.
She guarantees no crops will fail next year,
Halloween will be a local holiday,
a Friday the thirteenth every month,
and no curfew till cock-crow.
The voters are enthralled.
On Election Day it only rains
on her opponent. He's all wet.
Once she becomes the mayor
the budget balances like magic.
There is no need for taxes—

visitors in record numbers
feel compelled to spend their money.
Cats get a general amnesty.
The elderly dames of the city council
rock and nod and stir the pot
where politicians stew.
Everyone else is happy.
The mayor fingers her tarot cards,
studies a map of the Potomac,
reaches for a pin.

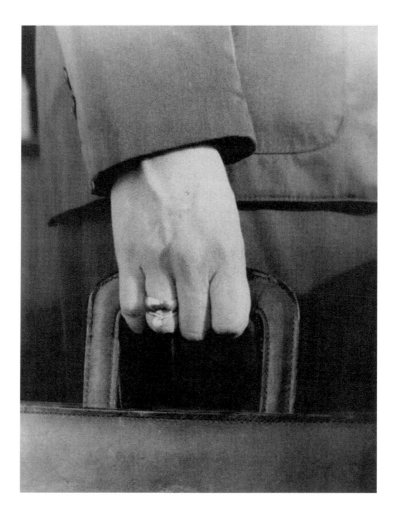

Photo by Marilyn Nolt

female executive

She rises early, in the shower,
coffee over, teeth pearly, blow dry,
powder, blush, line each eye.
Perfect suit for ambition.
Never trust to attrition.
Read mail, meet board, get the word,
call clerk, he brings coffee, pen, pad.
Answer mail, assess performance,
meet achievers, call home.
Lunch bunch, quickly munch.
Review reports, report to boss,
late to meeting, motivate,
call home, put out fires
that won't wait, call home.
Have a drink. Miss dinner.
After all these things are done,
she mothers her tiny one.

my ambivalence

He supports Women's Lib.
He's quick to point out they are underpaid.
It's not who holds the door open;
The real issue, he says,
Is money and power.
I agree: Form doesn't matter.
Sure, it's money and power.

When we leave he insists
       On his getting my coat from the hat check,
       On his taking my stub to the parking attendant,
       On my waiting in the warm lobby.
I wait and gnaw on my ambivalence:
       He's polite, why should that bother me?
       Why doesn't this feel right?
       I struggle to know.

When we play out our accustomed roles,
We can't see how the parts make up the whole,
How being put in the warm lobby also
Puts "No Admittance" on the boardroom door.

First I feel, then, slowly, I know:
What really matters
Is Money and Power and Who holds the door open.

prophecies

Women of the future will
design future sinks
with space behind faucets
so men can scrub the crud
without getting cramps
in their hands or
using their toothbrush.

Women of the future will
design ovens so that to bake
and to clean the stove
men don't have to squat,
kneel as to gods,
stick their heads in.

We will design vacuum cleaners
with long suction tubes
so men don't crunch
their spinal discs.
And supertight superquick
tire-changing kits
that work even on lonely roads
at night in the rain.

At least now that men
are washing more dishes
they've invented detergent
for sensitive skin.

My ex- learned to clean and cook
for his new lawyer-wife,
even to bake her bread.
That's progress.

she pours

WHAT ARE THESE CEREMONIES AND WHY
SHOULD WE TAKE PART IN THEM?
—VIRGINIA WOOLF

She has been told it's an honor
and knows that's a lie. Still, she sits, smooth as silk,
busy with sugar shell, creamer, and cup.
When she looks up, she smiles.
She has read Amy Vanderbilt's book
and knows to appear pleasant while pouring.
It's part of the art, like tilting the pot,
watching cascading brown rivers descend.

What she really likes asking is: One lump or two?
(a Three Stooges line, followed by a whack on the head)
What she likes hearing is: Half a cup, please,
which calls the Mad Hatter to mind. Now she is rising
abruptly, she is smashing the Doulton cup
and handing a half to the man with the diamond studs.
Her smile never falters. She climbs to the chair,
she yanks one rose from the florist's arrangement
and sticks it into her hair.

As she takes up the pot, the guests fall back.
The man with the diamonds cowers.
He's nobody's fool. He knows that power
can suddenly flow in a new direction.
His credentials are dollars—solid as steel.
Hers are liquid as tea:
Words surging, undammed, through her head,
milk that came down to feed her babies,
a once-a-month blood flow, red as the florist's best.

She is a brewing storm, pent up with things to say
while she chimes, Sugar? Cream?
Ideas tumble down her veins, out the tips of her fingers.
Over table and sconce,
over the house with its spout of a chimney,
all over the snowy damask town,
she is pouring, pouring.

biology is destiny

Dear Dan,

I really admire your persistence, but I worry about you. How will you ever get married? I'm an enlightened woman, but as soon as you open your mouth you alienate most people.

My friends are quite tactful since you're my brother, but it's easy to read their thoughts when they say, "Daniel is an unusual man, isn't he? So handsome. Does he always talk that much?"

Danny, do you have to be so strident about your views? Change takes time. Don't you think that you've achieved enough as a male professor at the finest school in the country? Do you have to apply for the position of dean? Another man, maybe—but you're known as a radical masculist. What chance do you have? I'm sure you haven't considered how the talk would affect the family. Don't care for myself, but Mother will be retiring soon as Speaker of the House. She doesn't need to cope with another round of debates about the Status of Men. Think of her heart.

But there you go, a typical man: act first and think of the consequences later, always after the rush of adrenaline. You men are
so emotional.

Now Dan, I can just picture you getting red in the face, steaming (which proves my point), but you have to admit that women and men are physically different. Even our brains are different. Didn't you see that special on the educational channel? Women think of many things at once and our brains are never at rest. Male brains can only focus on one task at a time and if not focused, the brain is off. Doesn't that show that women are naturally made for intellectual work and men for labor? Just look at your muscles.

I've heard you say often enough, and you know I agree, that machines and technology have liberated men from labor, and so men should be admitted into work that requires intelligence. But you have to be more patient, dear. Change takes time and we're going against nature's way. Many people are afraid that—with men leaving their traditional places in mines, fields, and ditches to engage in sedentary, intellectual work—community values are eroding. What will happen to all that pent-up male energy if it's not safely vented on chopping up rock? Have you seen the statistics on the increase in crime?

Not to mention your uncontrollable hormones. It wasn't that long ago that there was an evening curfew for men to prevent them from randomly assaulting women and turning order into anarchy. It was for your own good. The jails are rotting now with men who just followed their natural aggressive instincts without thinking of the consequences. What good has equality done them?

Now don't use yourself as an example. You're an exceptional man, even you must admit that. I won't deny that some men might be fit for the intellectual life, just as there are a few women more suited for the physical. That's why I support equal opportunity. If a man can do a woman's job, he should certainly be allowed to, but Danny, you're just confusing people when you tell them that their natural inclinations aren't good enough. Men used to be proud of being the laborers of the nation. They saw themselves as builders of the Pyramids. It didn't bother them that they weren't the designers. That task belonged to woman.

You'll say men just have to be socialized to govern their actions intelligently, but studies have shown that men respond instinctively to visual clues of anything that has the remotest resemblance to female parts. I can just imagine men in Parliament making decisions while looking at their coffee cups, their nether regions engorging. The very fact that men are so preoccupied with the size of their genitalia seems to indicate—well I don't want to insult you, dear, but the truth is it does indicate that nature intended men as breeders, not leaders of civilization. What other explanation is there for such an irrational fascination with a dangly bit of flesh?

You know what they say, "The cradle of civilization is in the womb," and "Man is brawn, woman brain." Just old sayings, but there's always a grain of truth in old sayings.

Be satisfied that your school has decided to offer a program in men's studies. I really haven't had time to look through all the books you sent me, but I did glance at *Men's Poetry Through the Ages.* That Willie Shakespeare isn't bad. Nice imagery and rhythm. Like many male poets he doesn't have any internal resources for meeting the world, but has to express himself through his love of a woman. How many sonnets did he write? But never mind, dear. As men have more contact with the realities of life, their literature will be more interesting.

I'm glad to see that you'll be teaching a course on History Through the Eyes of Man. A fresh perspective always casts new light on the facts. But don't lose sight of the facts dear. It's so easy for men to get lost in fantasy. Just like male cats hissing and puffing up their fur to look bigger when another male steps into their territory.

I can't believe that you, with your intelligence, actually believe that in prehistoric times men went out to hunt while women sat around the fire in a cave. Have you ever seen the size of Neanderthal Womens' bones? How often do you think those little Neanderthal men could have brought down a woolly mammoth to feed the tribe? The facts, darling. Remember the facts when your dear male brain wanders into puffing and hissing. We know that it was women who gathered roots and berries to feed the community of females and children, while men ate what remained, grubbing for insects and lifting boulders. It's fine that you're writing a book about the Naked Man Ape. You men should know your own history, but don't expect it to replace real textbooks.

I don't want to discourage your aspirations. You're my brother and God knows I love you no matter how much of a masculist you are. And who can tell, if you're right maybe She is a He.

But do try to put some thought into your actions sweetie, for Mom's sake if not yours. You can only stretch nature's design so far without tearing it apart.

Your big sister, loving as always,

Jan Cathyway

P.S. There's a new service agency called "Romantic Encounter: Mates for Unusual Men." I'm enclosing their brochure.

the glass ceiling

They call it "the glass ceiling,"
the barrier in business that women
cannot rise above. If it is glass,
sand heated to silk, it cannot last
long as ceiling. Our fingers know
the weight of bone china as we set it
lightly between silver. Our fingers
know to pinch shards of shattered
tumbler off the floor, from baby's toes.
Our fingers know, in frustrated dark,
cool air on the other side of the pane.
We have watched our mothers' hands
until our own hands learned
glass yields to patience.

hard times for women

Listing my chores for the day,
the decade, the next century, I note
that the planet needs saving—by
screaming, I suppose, out on
the street like a rabid banshee,
hoisting a placard, shaking a fist,
      when I'd rather ride by
      in a carriage, smiling
      and doing my queen wave.

I hate being jostled by bodies,
roared at, hassled, arrested,
going limp in debris—a disgrace
to my mother, a public nuisance
      —how often
      I'm told, and
      at times I agree.

If ever a man did as he promised,
to *cherish* the ground I walk on—*our*
earth—I'd never again stall his
traffic and hear myself cursed.
      I'd rather be home
      in my garden, pruning
      and pulling weeds.

Yet it's still the same as always,
whether wanting the vote or saving the
world, stopping a war, needing a pay
raise or care for the children,
      out in the street
      with my banners and bitches
      marching and going to jail.

a haiku for minister louis farrakhan, leader of the nation of islam, who called one million black men to washington for a day of personal atonement for abuses to the same black women the minister not only did not invite to the march, but whom he specifically asked to stay at home to pray, to take care of the children, and to make box lunches for the brothers

I can't stomach the
speaker or the message. But
here is your sandwich.

without permission

"We'll be there in two hours," Jolene tells her daughters in the back seat, cheerfully, she hopes, as she pulls onto the San Bernardino Freeway. How hard it was to decide to go off for a week, to tell him they were going rather than beg for permission. But he didn't argue. He's being careful. Staying sober.

A thunderous blur of cars to the left. Everything in her wants to brake, but she forces herself to accelerate and merge, signal and ease into the center lane. One thing about a freeway on-ramp, there's nowhere to go but forward. She remembers to breathe, wipes sweat-soaked palms, one by one, on her jeans, and smiles, reassuringly she hopes, at Lori in the rearview mirror. Lori, eight, is a worrier. Before they left, she checked the gas gauge, and Jolene expects her freckled nose to appear at her shoulder any minute to check it again. Nine-year-old Lydia is already recording the vacation on her drawing pad.

God, people must be insane to do this. Cars go seventy miles an hour inches away. Idiots change lanes with no warning. One false move and...no, can't think of that. To calm herself, she asks Lydia, "What are you drawing, honey?"

"Our house. So I won't forget how it looks."

"We'll be away only a week." Has Lydia guessed her life may soon change? Is it fear of change that makes her want to preserve the image of the yellow stucco house with the bird-of-paradise in front?

He's being careful. Maybe he thinks now that she's seeing a therapist he might lose her. Her mysterious sessions with this witness to their lives gives her leverage. For now. And she's not so alone. She wipes away tears. She cries often these days. Hard, choking sobs at the kitchen sink, blinding tears as she drives home from the therapist. Tears catch her off guard at work and she hides in the women's room. That's where Darla found her and offered the mountain cabin.

A truck passes, and she grips the wheel as if to keep the battered Toyota wagon from being sucked under. Tries not to remember the one other time she drove the freeways. But it was different then. He was in the car too, drunk and screaming directions: *Change lanes, damn it. Speed up. Slow down. What did you do that for? Don't hold the steering wheel so hard. What makes you think you can drive?* Two endless hours driving back from his friend's house in the Valley with their terrified children in the back seat. Because the girls were with them, she insisted that he, who never let her drive his car, hand over his keys. He gave them to her, finally, then to show who was boss, yelled all the way home.

A truck so close the windows rattle. She forces her hands to relax. Take it easy. Don't think about the mountains ahead, fear of heights, fear of the night. Remember what Dr. Luther said: *One step at a time. Break it to him in stages. Move him out. Trial separation. Get the gun out of the bedroom.*

"Do you have a map, Mom?" It's Lori.

"Right beside me." Does she sound too perky? Kids are so smart. "I have a map of San Bernardino County and a detailed map of Big Bear."

"Does Daddy know how to get there?" Lydia asks.

She glances at her oldest daughter. Blond curls imprisoned by a pink barrette. Long dusty lashes. Delicate but tough. What will make her feel secure: yes, Daddy knows where we're going, or no, he doesn't know how to find us?

"I guess he could locate us if he has to." She pauses. How can she have it both ways? "I mean, if there's an emergency, he can get Darla to bring him." She didn't actually tell Darla not to reveal her whereabouts. Should she have?

"Does he have a map?" Lori asks.

"No."

"Can he call us?" Lydia asks.

"There's no phone, but we'll call him every day." To make sure he's still sober. And what if he's not? Easy. One thing at a time. Act strong.

"How more long?" It's Lori, a mock whine couched in a favorite family phrase left over from her babyhood. Still, there's an edge of anxiety to it.

"Another hour." Almost through with the freeway. It's easier now to move along with high-speed traffic, although she still grips the wheel when trucks pass. She practices changing lanes, experiments with the fast lane. She can do this. This part of it, anyway. She's elated. "Does anybody have to pee?" She laughs at their surprise, revealed in the rearview mirror. What they know of vacations is long, cross-country trips, with catnaps alongside the road in the middle of the night. Lots of coffee and lots of coffee nerves. Grudging bathroom stops.

"I can wait," Lydia says dutifully.

Feeling giddy, she heads for the off-ramp. "Let's stop anyway."

Highway 30 winds through foothills covered with chaparral, then up through pine forest, up and up to Highway 18, where the road narrows and clings to the edge. One curve at a time. Show daughters this is no big deal. Act strong.

"I'm drawing trees now," Lydia says.

She stops at every turnout to let traffic pass and to gather courage for more switchbacks. Always this fear. Fear of heights. Fear of the night. Fear of *him*.

Lori peers at the odometer. "Are you going too slow for traffic, Mom?"

"No dear. Just enjoying the view." They get out at the next overlook.

"Look how far we've come," Lydia says.

Below, partly obscured by pines, a layer of smog hovers over urban sprawl. Her lungs expand in the clear air as Lori's hand clasps hers. She can do this.

Following Darla's map, she turns onto a dirt road that winds through the woods for half a mile, then pulls into a narrow driveway. Trees shadow the front of her friend's cabin and boulders rise in back. Protected, but dark and small inside. Quiet. Un-lived-in smell. She's glad they will have to share a bedroom.

By the time they finish the dinner dishes, the night sounds of the forest surround the cabin. She locks the front door, double-checks the windows. Decides she won't let herself recheck them later, as she does at home when he stays out late, going from front door to back, double-checking, rechecking, only to do it again in an hour. Never sleeping until she hears his car in the drive. Afraid. Of what? Just afraid. Afraid. Afraid. As if she's safe when he's there.

She lies in one of three narrow beds and asks herself who or what she's afraid of. It's quiet except for pines soughing in the wind and small animals snuffling about the cabin. Reassuring sounds. Surely they are reassuring sounds.

Lori doesn't think so and climbs in beside her and they make a game of naming the night noises of home: cars on wet pavement, doors slamming, dogs barking, gas heater clicking on and off, rain on the patio roof. She doesn't mention the hundred-and-one noises that sound like a lock being jimmied.

Lori sleeps and Jolene plays a game with herself called: What's the worst that can happen? Her mind veers away from it, then back. What if he takes a drink, then another? What if he comes here? Would he do that? Depends on if he feels as threatened as he felt when she drove his car. She flinches against the pillow as she remembers the flat slap of his hand on her face. She sees again his grim look as he hung his rifle above their bed the next day. Her shaking hands when she called the therapist. She gets up to check the door.

The next morning, she drinks coffee under a flawless blue sky. Shafts of sunlight cut through scented pines. She climbs onto a boulder almost as high as the cabin. She did get some sleep after all, more, in fact, than nights when she waits for him to come home. Maybe she can do this, too. Lydia appears in short pajamas with kittens on them. Her hair is mussed, but she looks tidy. She climbs the boulder and leans her head against her mother, and Jolene gathers her close.

"Can we go horseback riding?"

"Sure." Just now, she'd say yes to anything. Oh, the luxury of decision. Lori emerges, already dressed in shorts and a T-shirt.

"We get to ride horses," Lydia calls.

Lori looks at Jolene, wide-eyed. "Can we?"

"We'll see." She stares down Lori's do-you-know-how-to-ride-a-horse look. She does, and she doesn't. "I hear they use only horses that have forgotten how to run." She's not as sure as she sounds.

After breakfast, she watches the girls climb boulders, smiles at Lydia's lavender Keds and makes a silent bet they will still be clean at the end of the day. She recalls Lydia's face that night after the wild ride, after what came later, when she said to the silent, white-faced child, "Try to forget; pretend it never happened." After six months of therapy, she wonders which was most damaging: what Lydia saw that night or her mother telling her to forget. Because of her words, will she always have to guess what goes on inside Lydia by her drawings?

Later, they find a phone booth and call home. He asks solicitously if she's nervous without him there at night, and she says no. Resists asking why that suddenly concerns him. Lori gets on the phone and says, "Daddy, I get to ride a horse." Lydia gives Jolene a look that startles, a look that says Lori should have kept quiet, and when her turn comes, she doesn't mention horses. Jolene doesn't know which is the most disturbing, Lori's carelessness or Lydia's carefulness.

When Jolene takes the phone, he says, "What's this about horses? Did Lori make that up?"

"I told her we'd see." She has trouble breathing, as if a cord has tightened around her chest. The phone booth feels claustrophobic.

"Horses are dangerous, unpredictable. You could never handle one."

Anger takes her by surprise, but she chokes it down. Act strong. "I suppose not," she says, feeling unpredictable. But she avoids the girls' eyes.

She puts off the horseback ride. Because he won't let her or because she's just afraid? It's easier to blame him. They play miniature golf. Fish. Hike in the woods. Go on a sightseeing boat. Except for a mouse in the cabin one evening, there are no more night fears, and after the first three days, Jolene stops checking locks, sleeps like a child. The phone calls get harder, though. She watches the girls watch her anger veneered with false cheer. She doesn't want them to tell him anything; won't suggest they deceive him, but knows she has taught them to deceive. She tried to protect them, lied about where he was when he didn't come home, covered for him when he broke promises. Taught them to pretend.

Shopping for souvenirs, Lori says, "This is the first vacation we get to do whatever we want." Jolene feels happy, then despairs for all the times that should have been good. What went wrong? But knows she's beyond asking.

While the girls browse through knickknacks, Jolene drifts to a display of local art. Maybe she will buy a painting, one small enough to fit on a stand. He won't let her put holes in walls; anyway, he chooses furniture and wall decorations. She thumbs through a stack of watercolors, but a large oil painting catches her eye. Something about the way light plays on green. A mountain meadow. Wildflowers. A creek with lush ferns on either side, dappled with sunlight. Mountains behind. She's stunned by her reaction, by how the light, the green, the sweep of mountains, fills her with the joy of possibilities. *Valley of Fern*, it's called. She wants it as she has rarely wanted anything. She turns away, comes back, and an idea filters, like sunlight on fern, into her consciousness. Why not buy it?

"Mom, we're ready," Lydia says, holding a miniature kerosene lamp. "Like the one in the cabin on the shelf." Jolene admires it, and Lori's bronze horse.

"What are you getting for yourself, Mom?" Lori asks.

She turns to the painting, to the moment of decision. What will he say? Will he like it? If he doesn't, where will she put it? And what will her daughters learn from what she does? Anxiety crowds out excitement. Heaviness descends, like a hammer, familiar, yet strange because this week, for a few hours at a time, it's been gone. She pays for the girls' treasures, struggles to cover up her anger, fear, depression, so heavy now she can hardly bear it. But she must act strong.

In the car, the girls chatter happily, then they, too, become silent. How often does she shut them out while she shoves down pain?

Finally she's alone, in the woods behind the cabin where she can fight it to the ground. But it's as if something has come out of a box that was too small and now she can't stuff it back in. She drives to the phone booth. Anger drums from her fingertips and obliterates fear as she dials the number of the horse ranch.

She asks for three gentle horses, "the older the better," for the next morning.

Three teenagers and a family of four join them at the ranch. As she's helped onto her mount, Jolene fights down panic. She's forgotten how big a horse is, how far from the ground, that first sickening jar as the horse shifts its weight. She strokes the coarse mane and whispers, "Easy Betty." She's glad it's a mare, and is reassured by the heavy-lidded way the ancient bay droops her head.

Led by a young woman, they ride through a meadow filled with lupin and Spanish broom, then into woods where the horses pick their way up a steep sandy trail. Lori's face is a study in delight. Lydia grips her reins tightly, reminds Jolene of her own white knuckles on the steering wheel that first time on the freeway. Oh, for her daughters not to fear. She feels sick with anguish.

The trees recede and the trail broadens and they look down onto light dancing on green lace. Her Valley of Fern. They stop and look. No sounds but insects and birds and the creak of leather harness and the gentle blowing of the horses. She tells herself this is perfect peace, that it doesn't matter that she can't have its likeness, that she will take the real thing with her to relive when she needs it. But it's not enough. Her vision blurs, mists the valley with rage.

The trail descends, steeply, narrows to a single-file path. Jolene reminds herself that Betty picks her way over these rocks every day and will not stumble. Lydia is in front of her, behind the guide, and Lori has dropped back to ride with the family. Jolene envies the family, the parents' obvious shared delight. Was it ever like that for her? How did it happen that her marriage is normal only on the surface, at least until the weekend when he enters his own hazy world of drink, draws into himself, sullen. It's worked because he doesn't make demands on her when he's drinking, and she never crosses him. Except that once.

Suddenly, one of the teenagers whoops and spurs his mount out of line. Lydia's horse jerks its head and turns halfway around and she screams, "Mommy, Mommy, Mommy." Without thinking, Jolene calls out, "Don't let the horse know you're frightened." Lydia stops screaming, but the horse tosses its head and dances as if about to take off. Lydia hangs on, grim but determined, until the guide reaches her side and takes the reins.

"You did good," Jolene calls to her daughter. Her own voice trembles. She wants to embrace that rigid back and tell her to let the sobs go.

Like she should have done that night, after the freeway ride, after what happened later, when he left and Jolene climbed into bed with Lori and sometime in the night awoke to his shadow swaying in the doorway demanding breakfast. She rushed into the hall, afraid the girls would wake up, and whispered, no, go to bed it's late, but he said again, make me breakfast. He had never asked anything of her when he was drunk, that was the unspoken rule, but she had broken the rule first when she crossed him. She said no again, and the slap caught her off guard and she staggered and another slap on the other side of her head, and all she could think was this is what I've been afraid of, it's happening and all the strength was gone from her he was so strong and she wasn't and all she could do was say, "oh no, please, not this" and then Lydia at her elbow, eyes wide and blue above pink pajamas. His hand raised to strike her again, but his eyes went to Lydia and his face changed as if something inside snapped back in place and he dropped his hand and turned away.

Now, she remembers his face as he looked at his child, and she knows. Some of the fear she feels is not about him. It's her fear. He won't drive all this way to beat her in front of their children. He never hit her before that night because he controlled her through her own fear. He does not premeditate violence, and he won't touch her with them there. Not while they are this small.

Lydia rides quietly, the guide leading her horse, but when she's finally allowed to dismount, Jolene holds out her arms and Lydia runs to her and sobs, clinging. Lydia, who never cries, who is always brave. Strong beyond her years, but with the kind of strength that could some day break her.

"I'm sorry Mommy." Jolene feels the thin shoulders, the hair still baby soft against her cheek, and Lydia's sobs come into her and something loosens inside, something dark and hard expands, sprouts wings, escapes her breast to soar, like a giant bird, over the mountain, to hover there, over the Valley of Fern. And Lori, standing solemnly to one side, reaches out and touches her sister's shoulder. We are a family, Jolene thinks, we three.

Finally, the sobs weaken and she wipes Lydia's dirt-streaked face and says, "Come on, I still haven't bought my souvenir."

The next day, going home, Jolene drives slowly down the mountain and turns out to let traffic pass, but not as often as on the way up. She almost looks forward to testing herself once more on the freeway.

"Mom," Lydia calls from the back seat, "next time we go to Darla's cabin I want to ride a horse again."

She smiles in the mirror and nods. "Maybe we'll take riding lessons."

There's a local riding club. Surely someone there…

"Can we?" It's Lori, who has forgotten to check the gas gauge.

"Will you ask Daddy when we get home?" Lydia says.

She meets her daughter's gaze in the mirror. "I think we'll just do it."

When the forest ends and the chaparral begins and the air thickens with smog, the tears begin to flow. No sobs, just tears washing down her face. Tears for their own sake. Tears of release. The girls nap in the back seat so she lets the tears flow, relishes the cool clean wet on her cheeks, the salty taste on her lips. Feels a deep calm, as if a healing ointment is spreading over old wounds.

She's going back to the yellow house with its bird-of-paradise. She has no idea what the next weeks and months will bring. *Break it to him in stages. Move him out. Trial separation. Get the gun out of the bedroom.* Suddenly she knows the perfect spot for the painting. Over the bed. Tonight. She will be strong.

the power

Don't ask me what I'm thinking
as I stir the pots
and peal away the
fragile skins that hold me.

Wondering what's for dinner?
What's wrong now?
What I've done all day with myself?

Buried alive
is what I cried out one night.
A mistake, a misfit metaphor:
I am not dead.
Alive is something with a will
a power.

Want to see my powers?
Mother, goddess, writer,
witch, woman, magician
with a checkbook.
Wonder with a sick child,
a snow day, broken toy,
late meeting, forgotten lunch.
Enchantress of grocery aisles,
garden centers, day care, car repairs.
Famous laundress, poetess,
princess, painter of walls
pretty as a picture,
great pretender at parties.
Want to fight me?
I pack a wallop.

I want nothing.

tough

Tough
was your mother's word
for the kind of woman
she didn't want you
to become, someone
who didn't know her place,
who didn't know the game
rules, or even worse broke
them all, went after
what she wanted
openly, instead of playing
spider, weaving a web
that glittered innocence,
catching the morning
dew, the unwary
fly in the same
sticky threads,
surprised.

But you know tough
is the rock that takes
the water over and over,
becoming grooved but still
distinctly itself, the roots of
morning glories, honeysuckle,
that persevere and nurture
blossoms, Queen Anne's lace
and chicory that keep on
coming back in the haze
of the highway, in torn
up building sites, burnt
out lots, resilient,
tough.

the glass-smashing wall

The wall is broad and tall. It is for glass smashing, glass splintering, glass splattering, glass breaking. Any glass. All glass. Only women go. Cold, round, metal bars six inches apart join the bottom of the wall and stretch outward toward where the women stand. Large pieces of glass easily slip through the bars and drop the eight feet below. Glass of all textures, of all colors. Any glass. Only women go.

I watch women of many varieties at the wall, old and young, tall and short, fat and thin, poor and rich. All colors, all races. Some stand timidly and toss a cup or a small plate. They toss the object as they might a ball to a child, carefully, gingerly. Sometimes they turn around to see if someone might show annoyance at what they have executed, as if what they have accomplished is wrong. No one ever does. Rather, each woman accepts encouragement from the others to throw again, to throw with more force, to put her body weight behind the launch of the object. An ample supply exists of things to throw. Things the women bring, things brought at other times and left, things that shatter and splinter and break with a flick, with a lurch, or with a fling of the wrist.

The women line up away from the wall and approach one by one. While waiting they are quiet unless they feel someone needs encouragement. For example, Marian is next. She carries a large mixing bowl as she approaches the center of the wall, about eight feet back. She raises the white bowl over her head and as she thrusts her arms forward she yells, "No!" as loud as she can. The women, in unison and full voice, echo her "No!" When finished she steps aside and Gail glides to center. Gail carries two headlights that she excised from her husband's beloved Corvette that morning. He tends a liquor store in town during the day and sells crack in the city at night. He drinks and drives and goes to jail. Gail can stand it no longer. She extracted the headlights and hauled them to the glass-smashing wall. She lifts one and propels it through the air and she too yells, "No!" and the echo resonates. The second headlight follows the first and she jumps and smiles and is pleased with herself as if she has scored a strike with a bowling ball.

Alfreda approaches somewhat timidly and slowly, her ankles aching with sixty-five years of bad diet and ill-fit shoes. She carries a large terra-cotta flower pot she took that morning from her husband's garden. She dug the azalea from the pot and left the plant and its dirt by the front step. She told me she was throwing for all the years she had tended to that husband at his beck and call without any reciprocity while shoving aside a life of her own. She limps and the women heave a great sigh and worry that the weight of the pot might tumble Alfreda's body. She raises it and slowly slings it at the wall as she screeches, "No!"

Evelyn, whose husband abused her for years, follows Alfreda. Then Jennifer, who put up with unfaithfulness and lies until she could manage no more, then Lila, who is determined to take her former husband back to court to enforce child-support payments, and Susan, who just admitted for the first time to her sisters that their grandfather had molested her and they in turn admitted the same. And Jane, who trains male managers like herself but makes sixty-five cents to their dollar and Peggy whose husband of twenty-two years just left her for a younger woman. And Mary, and Willa, and Karen, and Agatha, and, and, and.

Betty approaches with a television set above her head. It has glass. Dangerous glass. When the tube breaks, it sprays shavings and chemicals. All the better. The risk. High risk. She puts the television set on the ground between her feet. She stands solid and contemplative before she bends at the waist. She touches the box on its sides and stands erect again, anticipating the weight on her arms. It is solid. She is solid. She bends again, grasps it, pulls it to her chest, heaves it over her head, back just about too far and suddenly forward until it crashes against the wall, noise and glass spraying. She retrieves the box and deposits it at the side of the glass-smashing wall.

The women hoist huge pieces of glass, large pickle jars or garden ornaments, lamp bases or umbrella bowls, lifted over their heads with arms stiff and feet anchored. Heaving, grunting, groaning, pushing the heavy item through space until the force splatters it against the wall.

I have been many, many times to the glass-smashing wall. I took my mother's wonderful and delicately constructed prewar crystal and slung it against the wall and listened to its soft tinkle, the same tinkle I heard years ago when one piece accidentally fell to the floor one morning as I lay in a half-sleep while pregnant with Natalie. I went to the glass-smashing wall with great heavy pieces, heaving, huffing, pulverizing, annihilating what I slung, what I launched, what I careened against the wall, delirious with strength enough to bounce the large objects, to watch them smash into small parts and vanish between the metal bars as I yelled, "No!" I went with all sorts of eating dishes, with cups, saucers, plates. I went with Italian candlesticks, with handmade flower pots, with porcelain, with terra-cotta, with carnival glass and tiles. I went at all hours of the day and night. I went in the middle of conversations about women and abuse, I went during films on South America and South Africa, I went in the middle of participating in intense arguments with my partner. I have been there with great armies of women pitching, groaning and heaving, dismantling, demolishing, destroying. I always leave strong.

I have learned glassblowing techniques. Skills that transform brittle and shredded pieces into liquid and back again into crisp and whole. I traverse the narrow stairway at the side of the glass-smashing wall and walk to the bottom, to the pit, to the place where the power is collected. I gather shreds from the pieces that the women so powerfully hurled through space, pieces that smashed and fell and collected far below and I toss them into the tremendously hot furnace in the corner, the furnace that transforms the ragged edges into smooth material that I collect at the end of my long blow iron. I poke the viscous matter with the iron and collect what the women have so valiantly discarded to free themselves of a layer of emotional encumbrance. I rotate the iron and tenderly blow my own life into the material to expand what is no longer fractured but what is hot and smooth and ready for a new life. Gentle breathe flows from deep inside my lungs, down the tube to inflate the mass at the tip to its natural capacity, to create a solid and stout piece. I create massive pieces, hundreds of objects of all varieties, small and large, symmetrical and lopsided, fat and thin. All colors, all shapes. The creations already line the outer wall of the large deposit room, some pieces pressed with bits of terra-cotta and tile, others smooth.

The large truck comes tomorrow and Bertha and Thelma will load the pieces to take them to Oregon and Mississippi and Washington, DC. Next week, Louise and Caroline drive to Montana, Wisconsin, and on to New York. Bertha and Thelma and Louise and Caroline will deliver the pieces, each resting on a bed of crushed colored glass, to be installed in Women's Centers, in galleries, in national museums, and many other places where women can touch them and feel their power and know about the glass-smashing wall.

after a while

After a while you learn the subtle difference
    between holding a hand and chaining a soul
And you learn that love doesn't mean leaning
    and company doesn't always mean security
And you begin to learn that kisses aren't contracts
    and presents aren't promises
And you begin to accept your defeats
    with your head up and your eyes ahead
    with the grace of a woman, not the grief of a child
And you learn to build all your roads on today
    because tomorrow's ground is too uncertain for plans
    and futures have a way of falling down in midflight
After a while you learn that even sunshine burns
    if you get too much.
So you plant your own garden and decorate your own soul
    instead of waiting for someone to bring you flowers
And you learn that you really can endure
    that you really are strong
    and you really do have worth
And you learn and you learn
    with every good-bye you learn...

mark her words

"I got a tattoo." My daughter Hilee's voice is like a child bouncing on the sofa. I press the telephone receiver closer to my ear.

"Where?"

"Don't worry, Mom, it's on my back. It's beautiful, a triangle with a woman sign inside."

"Did it hurt?"

"The pain is only temporary," Hilee says.

My younger daughter, Sarah, walks into the room and I tell her, "Hilee got a tattoo."

"Really?" She reaches for the phone. "What did you get? Wow, it sounds totally cool. Yeah, that's wonderful!" I listen to Sarah's excitement and I tell myself, "That is how I want to act next time." Then I worry, what if there is a next time?

"I want to know what will make you freak out the most," Hilee says, when she calls the next day. "Visible tattoos, face piercing, or scars?"

"Scars, tattoos, and face piercing, in that order," I report.

"I don't think I'm going to do any of those things, but I'll prepare you if I do. I want you to understand why this is so important to me," Hilee says.

Hilee already has scars that she inflicted on herself. She cut at her upper arms so she would not slice her wrists and kill herself. Her scars are symbols that she was strong enough to stay alive. This she explained to me several weeks ago. I look at the buds of pink skin on her arm and I wince at what she has endured. I look at the marks and I am grateful she knew how to keep herself alive.

Three years ago, Hilee came into my office and said, "I was sexually abused as a child." At that moment, my heart and my world stopped. When I breathed again, everything was different. My history was shattered, the family photos destroyed, and my image of myself as a good mother obliterated. Those words explained so much of my daughter to me.

My child was sexually abused…the thought haunts me. How can I forgive myself for not knowing? How can I accept that I didn't live up to the basic tenet of motherhood, to keep my child safe?

"Forgive yourself," my friends urge. "You did your best."

Hilee is undoing her hurt. She is stepping out and embracing her body. She pierces her labia, her nipple. She tattoos her back and dyes her hair blond. She reads about tribal scarifications and rituals designed to mark and honor the body. Every poke of the needle, every insert of color, is a step toward her true self.

Now I look at the nose and eyebrow piercings, the dragon tattoo on the cashier at the health food store differently. What used to be mere squiggles of color and pieces of silver, I now see as symbols, spelling out stories for those who can read them.

Hilee is teaching me to read them. I am slow. I resist. I cringe at the idea of my daughter being hurt.

"I was in pain before and had only misery to show for it," she explains. "Now I choose the pain and I have something beautiful and meaningful. I go right through the pain. Do you understand?" I breathe every word. I want to tell her she's done enough, she can stop for a while. I wonder how she can stand so strong and still, when I run from pain.

"I want to honor my Jewish heritage," Hilee tells me. "I'm thinking of tattooing 'Survivor' in Hebrew around my wrist. That way, I know I will never try to kill myself." Here is my child striding forward, transmuting pain into celebration.

Hilee's birth was my first real introduction to pain. My introduction to the fierce lioness love that never dims or dies; the love that can overturn a car or endlessly hold a crying child. Does that encompassing love include being excited and supportive about scarring, piercing, and tattoos?

I call a synagogue and ask the rabbi if he will write out 'Survivor' in Hebrew for me.

"Which survivor do you want?" he says. "Survivor, as in one left behind after a death, or the survivor of much trauma, like a concentration camp survivor?"

"The survivor of much trauma," I tell him.

For years, my daughter lived apart, her arms folded against me. Now she is opening to me, to herself, to life.

"I worry I spent too much money on this tattoo," she says, running her fingers over the triangle on the back of her neck.

"It's not really expensive when you amortize the cost over seventy years," I tell her. The tattoo hasn't quite healed; the woman symbol is puffy, swollen. I am amazed that she went by herself, bared her back to a stranger, and accepted this piece of forever.

"Isn't it gorgeous? Don't you want a tattoo?" Hilee asks.

Even when your child goes away for a long, long time, you wait. Every inhale is hope, every exhale despair. You go through life, working, smiling, talking, acting like part of you is not standing on the pier, staring out to sea, waiting for your own true love, your own true child.

My body is not decorated by needles or ink. This child is my tattoo, my indelible mark, my symbol that I lived through pain and into celebration. She is the story of my skin and my heart written all over me, for anyone, who is able, to read.

power

My power did not come sudden
like freeze that turns
calves to carcasses.
It was slow as land
before dinosaurs and flowerless
earth—earth that waits
for life's prints pressed
into its soil.

Mine is not the power that
bulges pockets, or curls
hands into fists
but the power of being
owner of my discovered edge.

Here, I place my back against
the wall not to guard myself
but to feel the stone's
damp shapes.
With my power, there are
no bad bugs in light-filled
cracks, only beetles that scurry
in mystic dance.
Soil reveals its glorious muck,
and color describes itself
at my every blink.

My power enabled me
to trade my loud silence,
that once beat against my soul
like a soundless drum,
for written words that speak
aloud and make me strong.

first behind the wall

The bulletproof vest chafing under my arms told me that I shouldn't be there. I was standing at the very edge of a building, too frightened to turn the corner, the first woman in construction at the maximum security prison, San Quentin. Not a desk job, not a protected position. They called this being behind the wall. And it was my first day on the job.

I had already peeked around the corner. Two thousand men were in the yard, enclosed by three stories of old stone walls. Maximum, I thought. For the murderers, thieves, rapists. They worked out with weights, their biceps gleaming in the afternoon sun. They crushed out cigarettes on shoes, on the ground, on body parts. I am a small woman, barely five feet tall, a little more than a hundred pounds, and men had never seemed so much larger, so much more powerful than they did that first day at San Quentin.

Hell, I had been through orientation; I'd learned the rules of behavior. The digital billboard just inside the employee entrance told me how many stabbings had taken place the day before and which racial group was locked in their cells because of it. Today all the African-Americans were in lockdown, so the yard held the northern and southern Mexican gangs, and the Aryan brotherhood. My new boss had told me to walk across the yard to the electrical shop in the other building. Clear a path through two thousand men, unescorted. Yeah, right. The yard was watched by the guys with rifles on gun rails and gun towers, but the guards seemed very far away.

I put my hand against the cool stone wall and closed my eyes. For a moment I was ten years old again, hoisting my old broken-down bicycle between my legs, hoping my shoes wouldn't catch on the peddles because they were my sister's shoes and didn't fit or because the soles were flapping loose. I'd start to feel safer the minute my butt hit the worn out springs and the frayed plastic seat. I'd peddle like mad, listening to the rattling chain, until the little dirt road turned into a desert with no road, no fences, or houses, cars or adults, no hairbrush that was beating someone back at the house. The wind would make the sides of my blouse billow out as if I were a kite. My sisters always hid under the porch, but I would fly through the desert, heading out toward red rock hills that I knew I'd never reach, watching the hot dust coat my bicycle, my legs, my broken down shoes, counting the crows and the lizards, past the rippled patterns of red and gold in the sand, the scant brush that looked like skeletons, the splintered rock.

My daydreaming, however, hadn't gotten me to the other side of the yard, and hadn't changed the sea of men into an expanse of harmless sagebrush. In fact, I was startled back from the desert by the blast of air brakes as a bus pulled up. I looked around the corner. Men were clambering off bleachers, jumping off railings with a purpose, a ferocious intention. They spoke to each other without seeming to move their lips; they threw cigarettes to the ground, stared at the bus from under crumpled, close-knit brows. The discord, the competition that could break into violence among the groups was something I had been schooled on, but today they seemed to move together, each of the individual gangs with the same purpose. Salsido had arrived. He was a local man who had gunned down his wife and his three kids. The men in the yard all faced the fence, then moving in slow motion to milk fear, the entire group of two thousand men moved step by step to the fence.

"It's wise to stand here for a moment," a voice at my shoulder said, and I jumped, then tried to recover my composure. "Just hold here for a bit," said a guard with his rifle held tensely over his forearm.

"What are they doing?" I asked.

"Makin' it clear that a man who kills his wife and kids is not a man. They'll kill him if he comes in here. Salsido'll go in with the perverts— the child molesters over in H Block."

I gritted my teeth. I thought of my mother, of the family reunions and the picnics, the birthdays where the women sat around coolers and paper-covered tables full of chicken watching men get drunk by the edge of the lawn. As the men's voices got louder, my mother and her sisters would take inventory: two children, purse under the chair with car keys in the side pouch, a casserole dish that's one helping away from being ready to go. Soon one man would shove another and somebody's brother would try to cool him down. My aunts would call their children away from that side of the lawn. If my aunts had been drinking too, they'd start shouting out derision, and then the draw would be too great and they'd march across the lawn one by one, the last ones to bring the first ones back until the whole family was shouting and flailing their arms, half of them trying to wrestle the other half into chairs. Grandma would brew coffee and act disgusted. The kids would get into the pie and steal money from their mothers' purses or dusty cologne bottles from Grandma's dresser. Somebody's car would break down or get smashed up and there would be kids sleeping on the floor of somebody else's house, and plenty of tales to tell of what happened to the ones who drove away and got into worse trouble later that night. I didn't like the sight of men huddled on the edges of things.

Supposedly, the men in my family had the same code: men fight with men. But we knew it was a code that only went so far. The women managed to stay out of the way most of the time, and marry the ones who got drunk and fell asleep before they got mean. Not Aunt Becky. There was a lot of hand-wringing and hushed talk at the kitchen tables. Then one morning they found Becky in the creek behind her house. The code had seemed pretty thin, then. Thin as the stockings she wore that collected the black dirt of the creek bed, thin as her wet dress that showed her slip and bra through, thin as the clumps of her hair that hung on the reeds and the water grasses. I don't remember much about how she died, except that my mother and her sisters plunged into the water, clutching at her and crying, dragging her up the creek bed and beating away any man who tried to help. They knew she had been killed just because there hadn't been a man around to fight.

It had been a rule that everyone had trusted, but suddenly the women in the family started fleeing like ducks in the fall. My mother's two sisters pooled their resources, moved to Austin, Texas, and got their kids into private school by working two jobs apiece. One of her brothers wound up in prison and everyone was relieved like he was a speeding train that finally hit a wall. Cousins got married, one got pregnant, one moved in with Grandma. Mother didn't speak to my dad for a week until one morning over pancakes he stood up at the head of the table, knocking his chair to the floor. "All right, I swear on my own goddamn soul that I'll never raise a hand to you." She made him write it down, and she hung the little slip of paper from a nail on the wall until it was brittle and yellow. My sister bought her a frame for it and it hung above her bed even after my father had been long gone, chased out of our lives by something that spooked him like he was a young horse with no sense.

In the prison yard, the men started stepping away from the fence. I saw them moving back toward their posts of bench, wall, bleacher. This was definitely not a time to be an interloper. I could see the guard tighten his grip on his rifle. After they've puffed out their chests and seen another man quaver, that's when men are the most dangerous. They're like dogs who have gotten a bit of blood on their snout. I'd never seen a fight that could satisfy them. Somebody else in the crowd would catch the scent, and there'd be another rumbling started elsewhere until someone put a stop to it, some cop or wife or oldest daughter and then they acted like dogs happy to be back on leash.

"I'm heading back to the paint shop," I said gruffly, making it clear that I wasn't to be dissuaded.

I didn't get all the way back, though. The men in the yard had too much blood in them and a fight broke out. I could hear the shouting. A rifle shot rang out and just like they had schooled us, everyone fell flat on their chests on the ground. The last thing you wanted when a guard started shooting was to be wearing prison blues and be standing. I was in the brown uniform of the "free staff," and I suddenly wished I were smaller, thinner, or could burrow under asphalt. You only got one warning shot, and then anyone standing was taken down. Guilty or not, they had a bullet in them someplace.

The sound of the shot echoed off the thick stone walls and ricocheted off the silence of snarling men who have been overpowered. There is no silence like it. In my aunts' houses, there was no day quieter than a Sunday when my uncles had hangovers. The kids knew to play outdoors, as far from the house as they could without getting into trouble. My uncles would sleep late, and when noon finally crawled into the windows and the shades were partly opened, my aunts would have been sure to be up just long enough to make it look like they'd been up a long time. Coffee would be served with a stare from under raised eyebrows. Toast would be delivered with one hand on the hip. Questions would be curt. The uncles would be pinned to the couch by the insinuations, the booze tearing at their insides. In each of the houses the tactic was the same. My aunt would raise her voice, knowing that the hangover was going to keep her man captive. He couldn't shout or hit when his head was pounding and his stomach was about to turn over. Guilt kept the sports channel at a decent volume. My aunts paraded up and down in front of the couch pointing fingers and leaning into their men's faces. We watched from the windows. The tone would get higher and more shrill as she tested his level of strength and determined that he would simply sink deeper into the pillows. Her hands would go up as she complained over the look of the apartment. Now was the time to bargain for the remnants in his wallet. In a good dress and an apron, looking like the model wife, my aunts would orate, testify, swear there was going to be a change in this house. Like the men flat on their faces in the prison yard, my uncles, the giants, had fallen.

The loudspeakers started blaring out instructions on which group of men should return to which cell block, and hesitantly, the previously swaggering men got to their feet and made sure they were towing the line before they moved a foot.

"You may as well go now," the guard said at my elbow again. I looked at him like he was a pesky child.

"Go with me," I challenged.

"Nooo," he said. "You'll just have to do it alone another day. Besides, then they'd know."

He was right, of course. Then they'd know. Couldn't have that. That was the rule even on the outside. My mother worked at a dry cleaner's when I was a girl. I hated to meet her there after school. The dry cleaner's was at the end of the main street, next to the bus depot, an old green building that looked like it had been a stable years ago. The paint was twenty years thick, and the screens on the windows were heavy and rusted. I could see her through a side window as she stood at the press, her arms all muscled-up and her shirt soaked through with sweat. She wore a kerchief that was dark around the hairline line and it made her skin look more tired, showed how bad her teeth had gotten. On the corner of a bureau at her side, in a little space not more than six inches across, she kept a picture of me and a plastic bottle of water. They sat on a little white hankie. I usually just looked in, then sat by the side window and waited for her, doing my homework in the dirt, or staring out at my desert that started at the edge of town.

One day I was trying to decipher my geometry when I heard her swear in pain. I jumped up and gripped the windowsill. She had a bright white jacket in the press, its icy cool sleeves hanging as soft as a fancy table cloth. Mom was holding her hand, then reached into the pocket of the jacket and retrieved something metal. It burned her again. She bounced it around in her hands to cool it, then quickly looked around. It was a money clip, fat with bills, and she smoothly slipped it into her pocket. I gripped the windowsill tighter in surprise. Theft was the way to true demise, my mother had always said. You can recover from setbacks, but you never get ahead when you've got a record. That day, though, she stood with her hands in her pockets, staring at the floor in front of her, considering the bills that were now hers.

Just then, a man in a very fine coat came in the door and Mr. Jacobson, the owner, barked a request for the white jacket. Mother slipped it onto a hanger and hung it on the pole in front of the man. The customer took one look at the jacket and started to grumble. There was a hole in the front fabric at the pocket. The cloth was still hot where it had been burned, they discovered, and the customer started demanding two hundred dollars for the jacket. How had this happened? Mr. Jacobson shouted at my mother. If she mentioned the hot money clip, she would have to give the money back, and worse yet, she would have to take it out of her pocket to return it.

Mr. Jacobson wasn't going to pay the man for his fancy jacket. Either he didn't have money like that or he wasn't going to part with it. He started hollering at my mother even though she had worked for him for six years. Jacobson looked back at the customer to see if he was appeased by the abuse. He was not. The man continued to demand payment for his jacket.

"That's it," Jacobson hollered at my mother, "I want you out of here!"

I ran into the store and slipped between them, stood by my mother's side. She looked down at me, took my hand, then took the kerchief off her head and put it in her pocket. Something washed over my mother's face that I had never seen before, and saw only a few times afterward. She stood mute, with her shoulders back and her jaw set. Jacobson could sacrifice her for the sake of a dinner jacket if he wanted, but he wasn't going to get her to beg for her job for the sake of his little drama. He would not know the truth; he and his fancy customer wouldn't know that she didn't know where else she could get a job in this little town, and he wasn't to know about the money that was the seed of her new plan.

"I'll expect my paycheck by the end of the day tomorrow," my mother said like a queen demanding a footstool. She walked right between the men and out the door. I grabbed her hankie and her picture of me and followed her.

The money clip had burned a circle on my mother's hand that turned into a scar, but the four hundred dollars it held got us into a better apartment and enrolled her in trucking school. It bought a revolver that she kept under the seat while she drove, and tucked into the waistband of her pants when she stopped for food. Weekends and summertime, I'd go with her.

In those days, she was the only woman on the road. "Where's your husband?" the truckers would demand, standing in a cluster around her. She'd put her hands on her hips in a way that opened her jacket to show the gun.

"Six feet under where he belongs," she'd say and use her elbows like battering rams through the crowd. Of course the truth was he was off somewhere, probably with some other woman, but the story didn't matter, we had gotten into the diner.

Today at San Quentin, I set my hands on my hips. This was a government job. For the first time in thirteen years as an electrician, I would make it through the rainy Christmas season without getting laid off. I would have dental insurance in a month, and hospitalization at the end of the day. I took a deep breath and walked across the yard. The men parted like water, their mouths gaping. They spit out toothpicks, they hiked up their pants, they folded their arms. But the sound of their insults and whistles were the sigh of my mother's steam press, the shrill cry of her air brakes. I heard women gathering pie plates and chicken tongs as men snarled in the background. I heard screen doors and the slip of women's shoes on the banks of a creek. I heard shrill accusations through a quiet Sunday morning, coffee cups hit kitchen tables, and doors that were opened for a peek at a child and closed again with relief. I heard small pans of food set down with great joy, and envelopes of bills that were shuffled and reshuffled in the hands of a woman who would come up with some way, somehow, to make them disappear. I was the first woman behind the wall at San Quentin, and as I walked across the yard, the catcalls of the men were the wind through my bike spokes in the desert.

city woman endangered

The sky had grown dark
but craving the night breeze,
I wandered outside
to walk the shadowed streets.
I gained energy,
as I took in the sights
of cats huddled under parked cars,
hoptoads crossing the road,
and neighbors pulling curtains
shut against the night.

I paused near the grassy strip
above the Kilmarnock Street bayou,
across from the railroad right-of-way.
I sat down in the weeds and grass,
aware that a woman
should not,
should never
idle in the wilderness
alone after dark.
My breasted form might betray me,
my long hair or silver jewelry
might signal woman, prey, victim.

Soon I stood up and walked on,
but for a moment I imagined
being able to linger there
gazing on nature,
and studying the night sky.
Yes, I could stay—if I had a gun.
I felt it in my hand, startling,
weighty, secure, an ugly thing,
a gun, a man's thing, so needed
to make me safe from men.

a fable of obeah women

There isn't anything in this village except a cluster of old obeah women. No tourist eyes have ever seen this place, and the locals only come when they have a spell they want cast. Most people would like to think that our powers aren't as strong as they actually are, but they are. That's how a group of old witches could put down their roots in these mountains without having to pay taxes or pay for our electricity or water. Yes, we have all those things. We got them without asking for them. One day the men in blue overalls came and told us they were giving us light to see by at night and water to cook by in the day. None of the other villages up past New Castle, high on the top of the Blue Mountain range, have water or light. But then none of the other villagers have roots that spread so deep into the mountain that they can pop out of the earth's surface way down by Spanish Town in the form of yam or green banana that's gone bad.

We obeah women have the power to spread our poisoned roots through the soil the same way a snake has the power to slide down the banyan tree and find its way into your house, walling itself up in the partition behind your bed, bringing you bad luck even long after you're dead. Some call our power voodoo, others witchcraft, some say we only know how to scorch evil into the night. But we only do these things when forced. Like when one of the men from your village might pass along this way and take one of our young women to be his bride for a night but without the proper ceremony, contorting his face into sad expressions as he leaves his filthy deposit between her legs, only to get up and go back to his wife without so much as a thank-you. Sometimes these same men stop in a village further on and take a younger girl of about twelve and forcing her legs to open wide, he opens her eyes to the horror that can possess a certain type of man.

There are young obeah women, or old ones playing again at being young, that men passing through here—and not aware of who we are in this village—will try and get on top of. I am an old one but if I don my blue smock, my sagging breasts ball themselves up again to stand pert and pretty and my sun-wrinkled skin smoothes itself out. On the days I wear my blue dress, I might take one of the older village boys to lie comfortably with me in my bed, but I only take one that is willing to come. That is how I differ from the men of hate that stumble upon our village. When one of the men that likes to sit on top of unwilling women finds his way into our village, we women, who have no blood ties to the survivor, gather in a circle and infect his seed with our own poisoned seed. Not too long ago we had to gather ourselves into the revenge circle. Only someone's mind must have been too strongly centered on revenge. Perhaps a sister of the affected was allowed to perform the ceremony, or perhaps even the girl herself wedged her way into the circle without any of us noticing.

On the very same day that the man raped Luciana he returned to his village and he plowed his own wife and she cropped nine months later. Our scent had passed to his village and one of the women elders recognized it instantly as his wife labored through her birthing pains. Knowing our scent to be a smell of death she lighted perfumed candles around the woman as she pushed. She rubbed her stomach with a balm of glycerin, mango strainings, and cherry tree rootings. The woman, even in her agony, sensed that these were all rituals done to ward off death. In the midst of her labor that to her had seemed unusually long and hard she just stopped pushing and once having made that decision she decided to stop breathing. She slipped into ghost form and took her unborn baby with her.

This story came to the women of my village on the edges of a black wind, a wind that brought with it fifteen days of mud-sliding rain. Whenever the thunder clapped and the lightning spread fire across the sky we knew another baby had died. The man's wife and child was just the first. Our water stopped running and the electricity was so strong it burnt out our lamps. On the last days of the rain the puddles began murmuring the names of the dead babies. We knew this was not to be a good sign. But our powers could not reverse themselves in the strong rain. On the day before the rain ceased we all smelled fire torches burning, a day before they even had been lit. It was our one warning of what the villagers prepared to do. Our village had begun to smell of our buried bodily waste and the water we had been hoarding smelled softly of blood. Those of us who still experienced a monthly running of blood felt a crusting form between our legs but no blood flowed.

On the last night of rain none of us could sleep because the wind howled in the form of wailing babies, but just before morning the rain ceased and a calming wind blew through the village, lulling us all into a cocoon-like sleep. As the sun got high in the sky and the water-soaked roses lifted their heads to bask in the glorious rays, we awoke to the smell of torch fires burning. At first we felt fear and clasped each other tightly around the waist. We knew the damage that men, who thought their village would be made heirless by a bunch of women, could do. But then we realized that as we went to touch our sister partners, in what we imagined to be our last embrace, there was an obstruction— something that kept our hands from firmly fitting around each other. Upon inspection we noticed tiny silk-like wings sprouting from the blades of our backs. But as soon as we called them "tiny" we looked again and noticed that no, they weren't as small as they had first appeared. Then suddenly they had grown until we looked again and noticed that they were indeed quite large. Luciana was the first to spread hers in the sun and we saw how perfectly symmetrical the design on each wing was. Bright ocean blues and the red of a poinciana dazzled us and made us cry with joy. As we saw the orange flames leaping into the air at the bottom of the hill and heard the villagers' mad chants we took flight, hoping to find a patch of oleanders suitable for a colony of but-terflies that were once wicked old obeah women.

womanpower

On the perimeter of night
I give orders to the sun
let there be light

and the sun
dog tired from exercising
in a claustrophobic run

obeys me realizing
earthspin and moonshine
depend on scheduled risings.

If I can move the sun
with monosyllabic words
if I can color dawn

if I can charge the world
if I can work hard enough
if I can imitate God

I can birth my own self,
control my life.

the woman who married

The woman who married
herself had waited three years for a
bridegroom. She sent engraved
invitations. Sewed her own gown from parachute
silk. Picked roses crimson as birth
blood, a church
reaching right up to God.

The wedding waltz, a bustle of old
satin bridesmaids. Her veil
trailed down the aisle like saltwater
tracings abandoned on sand.
The woman gave herself
to herself.
Held her gold ring heavy in her right hand,
slid it down the chosen
finger on her left.

She turned to face her friends:
I do. I take it all
now. My sickness and health, my better,
my worse, both here and beyond
our idea of death.

You are, the priest said,
ah, one.

The crowd standing round
echoed his *ah* as she cut her own cake
crowned with a porcelain bride.
Drove away in a streamered
car to her honeymoon
house by a sea. Opened boxes of china
so fine she could hold
a plate to the light and see her own
life beyond.

to my lover

Yesterday was hard. Your words hurt. I found myself wanting to protest, to argue with you, to persuade you that your view of our relationship was "wrong" and mine was "right." I felt wounded and my mind played scenes where I flung harsh words at you, still intent on defending myself.

This morning I woke with that leaden feeling of "What's the use?" and went to the gym to see if I could work myself into a better mood and find something to lift me from the ongoing inner dialogue of woundedness.

As I jogged on the treadmill, I glanced up at the TV screen where a soundless drama took place based on "The Miracle of Fatima." Remember the story? Three children in a poor Middle Eastern village saw a vision of Mary, who revealed certain predictions that supposedly came true, to the astonishment of everyone in the village. Mary appeared to them twice more and in the final vision she told them things about the "end time" which she warned them not to reveal until later. Despite the threats of the local priest and the cajoling of parents, the children were steadfast: they would not reveal what they had been told until the proper time.

The movie was not a spectacularly good one. It was made in the years when cinematography was just beginning to explore possibilities for cre-ating "talkies" and still depended more on visual expression than on dia-logue to carry the plot. At any rate, I didn't miss the dialogue—every-thing was clear as I watched the beatific faces of the children, the mysti-fied faces of their parents, the confused, frowning, or pleading faces of the villagers.

As I jogged on, the children climbed the hill to receive the vision of Mary. Suffering village people—the blind, deaf, lame, poor—lined up below them, hoping to catch a glimpse of the Holy Mother or somehow to reap the benefits of such a sacred moment. I saw a man on crutches crying out, wanting to be healed of his afflictions. Then the camera flashed to the faces of the children as they stood transfixed, wrapped in the vision only they could see. I thought, "If only that man could realize that he already has everything it takes for a perfect life—to cure himself—from the blessings bestowed not just by Mother Mary but by all of life around us. If he could only see that he has a choice about how he lives life!"

That's when my epiphany came. I saw that I was that man. I, too, could have available to me all of the joy and abundance and transforming vision of this life, simply for the choosing. Like the man in the biblical story, I could throw away my crutches—stop relating to you out of a sense of being the victim of whatever you wanted that I didn't want—and walk on my own two feet, content in my own healing vision.

I saw that you and I could, together, create the relationship of our dreams, unfettered by the need to have it fit into any previous mold of who was "right" or "wrong." I saw how limited my own reactions were, and how my spirit could expand beyond them to embrace all sorts of new possibilities for us. Like the children lifted above the villagers' concerns by their hilltop vision, I knew I could never again play the old controlling games from my new perspective.

So, my darling, here I am, having healed myself from my self-inflicted ego wounds, declaring myself once more to be ready for whatever comes next with you. With us. And thankful for the powerful place we provide for each other to shape and reshape our love.

telling my father

Sometimes when I'm sitting at my desk trying to imagine the next word or phrase, I put down my pen and listen. Underneath the everyday noise—blinds rattling in the breeze, phones ringing, and voices murmuring or rising in anger—I hear the other writers. I hear pens moving smoothly on paper or scratching it; I hear typewriters being banged and paper rolling through them. I even hear the gentle blips of computer screens and the soft taps of keyboards.

I listen and conjure the faces and bodies of those who are making this din. There are hundreds of thousands of us sitting in a variety of postures, muttering or smiling, swearing or sweating as we force our minds to release the words we say we need to speak. After a while, I put my hands over my ears and try to stop the sound. My breathing gets ragged and shallow. I pick up the pen again, clutch it tightly until I'm focused only on the pain occurring between my fingers and in my hand.

When I am released, I return to my story. At night in my home, I ask my lover if she can hear mathematicians creating formulas or finding more of pi's eternal fractions. No, she laughs, we are the strong, silent nerds. Then she rubs the back of my neck and asks me again to describe what I hear when I'm not writing.

I could say it's a stone's long fall into a well, or the incipient cough at a concert that threatens to make its own rhythmic line. It certainly isn't a whole story that I hear or even a distinguishable voice. I hear words spattering pages like grease hitting the hot griddle, and worse, I feel the need that accompanies them. This recognition of our mutual condition brings me a dangerous despondency. So many stories pressing in upon each other. A hundred thousand lines trying to break lifetimes of silence and layers of denial.

How many make it through I wonder. And then Kate will draw me a formula that suggests (to her anyway) that my despair is misplaced, that indeed, given the numbers of magazines and journals and newsletters and friends of writers, quite a few of these urgent lines are appearing someplace at any given time.

And anyway, she'll say to me, isn't the most important thing that you write it down? The act of writing is what liberates, not the publishing. Even if it's published, you can't assume that you'll have sympathetic readers. You have to remember your purpose: what is it you want the story to do? Besides tell the truth, that is.

This is the part in our discussions where I sigh. Kate has such a romantic view of writing. She thinks that suffering is inevitable but salutary, that love does always come in time, and that telling the truth is as important as the truth itself. Terms like "sins of omission" and "white lies" do not exist for her. I envy her abilities to scrape away the drama, separate conflicting loyalties, and ignore the baggage of the past in any situation, concentrating instead only on the truth. I comfort myself that this same talent is what prevents her from writing stories.

And yet the irony is inescapable: I sometimes can't write the stories because of the truths they bear. And when I reach this point in my ruminations I always think of my father since it is he who first got me riding the merry-go-round called truth.

He was my first friend, my first teacher. In reading to me, he taught me how important rhythm and tone were to a story. Whether he was reading Uncle Wiggly tales to terrify his delighted young ones or helping me prepare MacArthur's "Duty, Honor, Country" piece for a high school civics project, he made sure I understood that words alone tell only half the tale.

He pitched endless baseballs until I could switch-hit and make running catches from the outfield like Mickey Mantle, my other hero. In such a way, he ensured I kept my neighborhood eligibility long after the other girls were dismissed. We spent summer evenings watering and harvesting the tomato plants he loved. He tried to help me with my math, but gave up in frustration over the new jargon and my inability to learn either the teacher's way or his old-fashioned methods. It was perhaps our first experience of me "acting like a girl."

My only brother appeared when I was four; he represented the first real challenge to my primacy with my father. I didn't count my sisters; they were ordinary girls obsessed (to my continuing bewilderment) with dopey dolls and useless dresses; my father and I loved them, sure, but we didn't spend a lot of our time with them. Raymond, however, meant I was going to have to share.

In the beginning, Ray and I became playmates. We wrestled and fought and ambushed one another every chance we had. He made up in intensity what he lost in size. A friendly shove soon gave way to real punches. We mostly kept it clean—no biting, no clips below the belt line—but inevitably someone's threshold of pain got crossed, and the screams brought one parent running.

As the older combatant, I was supposed to have known better. Every adult in my world seemed to know this rule that described an absolute relationship between age and culpability. I, of course, protested the rule, but honesty compelled me to admit it had worked in my favor with my older sisters. Now, however, as the "older" child, I grew resentful that every scene involving me and Ray led to my banishment and his restoration. Ray no doubt remembers this differently; let him tell his own story.

One day I was caught in a major transgression. I no longer remember the exact sin; I can, however, recreate the fear with which I stood before my father. I knew that I was in big trouble. He was in the living room sitting relaxed on the couch. I tried to leave several yards between us, but he called me over to him. My father looked at me with a mixture of disappointment and anger as he asked me if I had done what I was accused of doing.

In my fear I said no. My father pushed himself forward on the couch so that he was closer to me. He made me look at him directly. He spoke of truth and lies. He described the liar as someone others would shun. He said that lying starts with a simple, small falsehood and then becomes a habit until the liar no longer can distinguish the difference between what is right and what is wrong. He reminded me that one who tells the truth sleeps easily, fears no one, never worries about changing his story for every new audience.

"Now, pal," he said almost kindly, "I'm going to ask you again, and I want you to think about one fact: the truth is always the best way. Did you do it?"

It is nearly twenty-five years later, but still I hear my heart thudding and see my body shaking as I fight for enough control to be able to answer him. He sits easily, his face expressionless, his eyes relentless in their capture of mine. I start to explain what happened, but he holds a hand up to stop me. He repeats that he simply wants me to answer his question.

I drop my eyes as I gasp out a yes; he says he cannot hear me, I must speak up. I am looking at my feet so I only half see the movement of his arm which occurs simultaneously with my affirmation. Whack. His hand cracks the left side of my face, and I stumble a bit starting to cry, more from the fear than the pain, although it does definitely hurt. My father grabs hold of my right arm.

He actually says something to the effect that slapping me hurts him more than me. He tells me he is very sad because he has heard me lie and there's nothing quite so bad to him as a lie. He tells me to go to my room and think about how it's always better to tell the truth. Then he frees my arm and I dash for the safety of my bed where I can safely scream and cry like a girl, in my pillow.

I gave myself a massive headache, and while waiting for its dull pounding to subside I did think about my father's words. But I couldn't move beyond the paradox that telling the truth did not feel good. It wasn't ennobling, and it certainly didn't erase fear. Furthermore, the truth for which I was being punished wasn't even my truth. I had a different story I was not allowed to tell; the simple yes or no my father demanded did not allow for other aspects of the incident. Weren't they true too?

At the same time, I knew that I was guilty, both of the original deed and the attempted lie. My father's anger was justified, his blow a swift confirmation of my guilt. My father had no doubt about right and wrong. Why did I? It was confusing.

The immediate result of those thoughts was remarkable: I would not apologize. Usually, the ritual was for my father to offer friendship again; I would accept eagerly and apologize, solemnly promising to try harder in the future. We would shake hands and hug, and I would continue to see the world through his eyes.

But not this time. When he appeared at my door, I accepted his hand in silence. He asked me if I wasn't sorry. He seemed amused when I asked him if he was sorry for hitting me before I could tell him the whole story.

"I heard the part that I needed to hear," he said.

"But not the part I needed to tell."

And that's when I first began to understand that truth has as much relationship with who's in charge of the story as it does with some presumed absolute. As I grew older, telling stories assumed a greater truth: power over others' attention; knowledge that people waited for me to give shape to what they had experienced. And if I exaggerated some details and created other entirely fictional ones, no one complained. My new story made both participant and listener laugh, even as it pronounced them innocent or guilty. Such pretension, such ego; I plead youth and still admire the arrogant innocence of those years.

Falling in love with Kate, however, has meant a real confrontation with truth. At first, like any new lover, I simply ignored whatever proscriptions came our way; lust was so easily stronger anyway. I told myself that who (or what) I was had little to do with whom I loved. Kate was introduced to the family as just a good friend. When we moved in together, the family agreed it only made sense to share rent. But then we bought a house; the family wondered whose name was on the mortgage.

Their eyes slid from side to side when I told them both names were on the deed.

I could not get angry with them for their uneasiness. Something similar seemed to happen to me when I tried to say aloud what it was I said so often in my head—I love Kate. I told Kate that I was scared, that maybe I was more coward than consort. She assured me that I would find the words I needed to match the life we were living. It's two sides of an equation, she said, or a reciprocal, easier to see than to explain, but it always comes out even in the end.

I was writing stories all this time so I kept banging into the imbalance I had created. The "she" in my story was not always telling the truth. And my father seemed to be right; she didn't feel too good about it. She had to keep changing the story to satisfy the audience. And I could hear those other writers, insisting that we labor in order to say what really is true.

So, I've come to my parents' house, and I'm standing in front of my father who is reading on his couch. We exchange the usual pleasantries about the weather and my job, our nonchalance absurd next to the monologue running in my head. Standing over him like this doesn't seem quite right either. I bring in a chair from the kitchen and sit facing him.

"Dad," I interrupt myself, "do you remember telling me about how important it is to tell the truth? We were right here, and you said there was nothing better than the whole truth all the time."

He's laughing as he puts down his book and folds his glasses carefully into his shirt pocket. "No, but I'm sure I said that and just as sure I wouldn't say it now."

That stops me. "You wouldn't?"

"I think there's entirely too much garbage being spouted by people today. People telling each other much more than we want to know. There are no surprises anymore. When your mother and I married, it was the first time I knew that she liked black silk. You probably think I'm crazy, but boy, we had fun those early months just finding out stuff."

"Mom wore black underwear?"

He leaves his reverie to return to me. "Never mind, young lady, that's stuff for us to know. It's what keeps us us and keeps you you. We love you kids, but we're us first. It's been thirty-seven years, and when I say 'we' I still mean your mother and me. Do you know what I'm talking about?"

I take a full breath. "Yeah, I do, Dad. It's like me and Kate." And I'm willing him to keep his eyes on mine and willing me to keep my voice steady. The moment holds, expands, goes beyond arbitrary units of time. We're looking at each other with an intensity I've never known with him. His gaze travels to my right hand which I notice has become a fist.

"Are you going to hit me if I say the wrong thing?" His face shows the glimmer of a smile.

"I seem to recall that as a possible response. It would, of course, hurt me more than you."

And as he laughs, he stands and holds out his arms. I'm standing inside the circle they make, thinking that this truth feels good, feels right, is best. I'm in charge of the story, you see, and I'm as free as ever he promised.

alter ego

There is a nun with
a great bird headdress
who trails me through the streets
relentlessly—white wings
pursue me, black robes whisper
at my back. On the heels
of my taut step
I sense her modest glide.

She doesn't speak, offers
neither prayers nor comforts,
attempts no hindrance
to my worldly round
as she sails
the wintry pavement,
her ebony robes unfurled.

As my step quickens
she moves faster,
black brushing my footprints
on the busy street.
I feel her gaining on me,
wings flapping furiously—
I check my watch and hear her
singing psalms.

woman of god

Woman of God
I watch the people turn their eyes
to follow in their worship where you lead.

You come before the people with God's word
speaking the message that your heart has heard
a voice of vision from a life of faith.

You stand before the people, breaking bread
inviting all to "come, come and be fed,
take all you need and go away fulfilled."

You move among the people sharing peace,
a double blessing as you share yourself:
God's grace made real in handshake and a smile.

You walk among your people, filled with love.
Warm ministering presence, caring touch,
you reach into the lives of those you serve.

Sometimes I watch you, mystified
not knowing if I sense the God-through-woman
or simply woman, from a side I've never seen before.

Pastor—or sister—am I drawn to human love
or to the glow of Spirit shining through?
Woman of God,
I thank my God for you.

the traiteuse

The traiteuse was dying. Though Estelle had not spoken with her sister in twenty years, she knew Marie was dying. It was a small town; everyone knew.

Newly laid gravel splattered, plinking irregularly against Estelle's beige two-door Ford. She stopped completely at each intersection, monitored the speedometer to guard against exceeding the thirty-mile-per-hour limit, and wondered whether Marie had changed much. She was dying, after all.

Promptly at 10:30, Estelle arrived with her three-year-old granddaughter, Ti-Rose, who'd been running a high fever for almost two weeks. Estelle, as sister of a traiteuse, a healer, was entitled to free treatments. Marie would never deny her that, not after twenty years, not after twenty thousand years. She hesitated only briefly at the front door.

Irene, Marie's goddaughter, answered the knock. "She's been waiting for you," she said and led Estelle, Ti-Rose slumped over her shoulder, through the parlor. The gold brocade drapes were drawn so little light penetrated the room. One corner, where the sofa once stood, was empty, making the room seem incomplete, desolate. From the parlor, they quickly crossed the kitchen to enter a hallway on the left, where they passed two closed doors. Bedrooms, Estelle remembered. The hall ended at a door opening to the sun porch which was enclosed on three sides by floor-to-ceiling glass. Estelle blinked several times, her eyes adjusting to the room's startling brilliance. A rose-patterned sofa bed, an oak nightstand, and a stuffed chair, upholstery matching the sofa, were the only furnishings. The room smelled of camphor and sickness.

"So, Estelle, you've really come. I wasn't sure you would." Marie tapped the stuffed chair in invitation, then turned to her goddaughter. "Coffee?"

Irene nodded, then left the porch.

"You look good," Estelle said. Marie, already small-boned, had shriveled with disease. Her long, fragile fingers were attached to frail wrists, the skin stretched translucent and covered with blue feathery suggestions where dark veins once ran. But her face still held its pleasing round-ness, perhaps compensation for the suddenness with which illness attacked and doomed her to a quick death. Her grey-streaked blond hair was coifed in a bun at the nape of her neck and a touch of makeup colored her face which had always been too pale. The lilac gown comple-mented her violet eyes. She looked regal, stretched on the opened sofa bed. Estelle could almost forget she was dying.

"Can't look that good," Marie said.

"I didn't think you would. But you do." Estelle's honesty was partially provoked by her suspicion that Marie knew the truth regardless of whether a person told it. "So what else is new? You always looked good. I had to work just to look presentable."

"You looked good enough to have plenty of young men hanging around, as I remember. Plenty more than Daddy wanted, for sure."

Estelle smiled, remembering her father's chagrin at the appearance of each new suitor. As a teenager, she'd thought her popularity fate's way of apologizing for not making her a traiteuse. Marie had the gift, she had admirers. But Estelle knew, even then, she was not the lucky one.

"I'm not here to argue. Like I said on the phone, it's Ti-Rose." The child stirred briefly in her grandmother's arms at the mention of her name. "Medicine isn't helping. Her mother didn't think you could do any good. I told her you couldn't hurt either. I begged and pleaded and finally, to shut me up I think, she let me bring Ti-Rose. She would have come herself, but we thought it best the other children not come, what with you being sick and all."

"Dying, Estelle."

"OK, OK, dying. Anyway, with the circumstances and all." Estelle flushed. "We decided it best I come."

"Bring her to me."

Estelle carried the sleeping child, her brown limbs limp, to the sofa bed so Marie could rest her fingertips on the burning forehead. Slowly, Marie's fingers lightly massaged up to the small scalp and around the child's head. She recited French incantations taught to her by her father who had learned the words from his mother who had learned them from her father who had learned them from his mother, and so it had been for hundreds of years, long past the time when anyone could remember the first healer in their family, the first who had received the gift and accepted the power. The prayers would die with Marie because she had no son to teach.

Estelle sat in the chair, her eyes closed as she listened to the soothing rhythm of Marie's voice. Like most Cajuns of her generation, she spoke French fluently, so the words were old friends. But Estelle knew she could never have remembered them in proper sequence to be a traiteuse who must know thousands of words combined in intricate ways for a multitude of occasions.

Perhaps it was only Estelle's imagination, but Ti-Rose seemed almost comfortable when Marie finished. Estelle stood to pick up her grand-daughter.

"Leave her be," Marie said. "She's resting fine. Besides, Irene will have the coffee ready soon."

As if on cue, Irene entered carrying a silver tray crammed with a steam-ing coffeepot, two cups and saucers, a cream pitcher, a sugar bowl, and a plate piled with chocolate chip cookies. She set the tray on the bed-side table.

"You'll love Irene's chocolate chips," Marie said, smiling at her god-daughter.

"Call if you ladies need anything," Irene said.

"Seems like a nice girl," Estelle said.

"Nice for me," Marie said. "No one wants to die alone. Not even a traiteuse."

Estelle couldn't think how to answer that, so she said nothing. The grandfather clock in the living room chimed the hour. After a long silence, Marie asked, "Does Father Mouton know you're here?"

"I wouldn't be here, if he knew. He would've talked me out of it. You know that." Estelle stirred her coffee with her index finger, a nervous habit acquired during childhood and never abandoned.

"I suppose I do." Silence again. Then, very quietly, "It's a gift from God. It would be a sin not to use it."

"Father Mouton says—"

"I know what Father Mouton says."

"Maybe he's right and I'll burn in hell for bringing this baby here," Estelle said. "But, God forgive me, I had to do something. She could be dying. I had to try everything, even you. God couldn't think that was wrong, could he?"

Marie shrugged. "You know what Father Mouton would say."

"I know."

"Still you came. I'm proud of you, Estelle." Marie reached across the sofa bed to pat her sister's knee. "Are you ready to admit priests don't know everything?"

"Don't be sacrilegious. Priests don't pretend to know everything."

"Father Mouton does."

"Priests don't pretend to know everything," Estelle repeated, louder this time. "But they know about God and right and wrong and the devil's work and what a body has to do to stay out of hell and get to heaven with as short a stay in purgatory as possible. They know because they are God's chosen workers and the rest of us are supposed to listen to them and I haven't and God only knows the price I'll pay for coming here."

"I thought you'd gotten some sense into you when you called about Ti-Rose." The child moaned softly, then rolled from her back to her side, assuming a fetal position before quieting. "Guess I was wrong."

"Don't be mad, Marie. I never wanted you to be mad." Estelle stared at her coffee cup. Her finger stirred faster.

"How am I supposed to feel when my sister practically spits in my face for twenty years?" They both stared at the small child lying tranquilly next to Marie, as if neither wanted to chance looking at the other. "I expected other people to act that way, but not you." Marie's voice was so low, Estelle had to lean forward to catch the last words.

"Father Mouton was only doing the right thing. He didn't mean harm," Estelle protested.

Marie's tone lowered an octave, imitating the booming voice of the parish priest. Her voice lilted with his remembered cadence. "'Stay away from traiteuses or God have mercy on your erring souls.'" Her pitch returned to normal. "Meant no harm? Of course he meant harm—to me."

"It wasn't easy for me either, you know," Estelle said.

A faint breeze blew outside. The sisters watched the row of Easter lilies, planted along the property border, wave in near-perfect unison.

That Sunday twenty years ago, Marie and her husband, Clabert, had sat in their accustomed pew, second from the front of the church in the right-center section. The Virgin Mary, St. Joseph, and the crucifix were draped with dark purple cloths, symbolic of Christ's impending sacrifice. In keeping with the somber occasion, the main and side altars were bare, not holding the usual festive flowers.

When it became apparent Marie was to be Father Mouton's sermon topic, Clabert reddened, then whispered something to her. She slowly shook her head. Estelle had hoped, sitting three rows behind them, they'd leave. She should have known better. Marie wouldn't let anyone, not even a priest, chase her from God's house.

Estelle was certain the murmurs, which followed the end of the sermon and preceded the offertory, were all about Marie. Gossips would not be able to control their tongues until Mass ended.

Later, Marie slipped past Clabert to the church aisle, joining other parishioners walking to the altar rail for communion, the holy meal meant only for persons who were right with God. Estelle was too humiliated to dare ask for communion that day. Not Marie, though. She wasn't easily intimidated, even by a priest. Estelle could have died the way Marie stared at Father Mouton when she reached the altar, daring him to deny her the host. He did not confront her directly by refusing to serve her the communion bread. Instead, he placed the wafer on her tongue, quickly snatching his hand back as if he'd been burnt. Marie carried a small, triumphant smile back to her pew.

Everyone knew Estelle was the sister of a traiteuse, related by blood to a blasphemous, devil-worshipping sinner. That is not how she would have described Marie, but then she was not a priest. She fingered her rosary beads and prayed church would end soon so she could escape. She slipped out the side exit as Father Mouton raised his arms above his head, his back to the worshippers, giving his final benediction.

Father Mouton called soon after Estelle arrived home.

"You must set an example," he said.

"But, Father, she's my only sister."

"She's a traiteuse first, your sister second. Your soul is as muddied as hers if you continue seeing her while she's practicing. Give her one more chance. If she doesn't reform, cut the ties. It's your God-given duty."

That afternoon, in the midst of a lightening storm, Estelle phoned Marie and begged. "Give up the treating. Do it for the salvation of your immortal soul. Do it for me."

"That's like asking me to cut off a hand or gouge out an eye. God doesn't want us to mutilate ourselves like that. I'm not doing it. Not for Father Mouton." She spat his name. "Not for you. If the power were yours instead of mine you wouldn't give it up either. I would share the gift, if I could. But I can't. I also can't give it up."

"But it's your soul."

"Don't waste time worrying about my soul. It's in fine shape, thank you. Probably better shape than Father Mouton's."

Crackling lightening punctuated Estelle's sobs. Her stubborn sister was damning her sweet soul to hell. When she caught her breath sufficiently to talk, she whispered, "You heard Father this morning. I'm not talking to you until you stop your evilness."

Marie broke the sun porch silence. "Waiting until I'm dead before seeing me again?"

"No," Estelle replied, sighing. "No point to staying away now. I'm guilty as you. I've broken my promise to God and Father Mouton. All I can do is pray for forgiveness and I can't do that until I feel sorry for what I've done, which I don't. So, I guess the first thing I'll have to do is pray to feel sorry."

"Want to know a secret?" Marie asked. She leaned across the sofa's armrest, closer to her sister. "I had more clients than ever after Father Mouton's sermon. It was better than TV advertising. People I'd never seen, and who'd probably never heard of me before Father Mouton's preaching, came for help." She paused dramatically.

"Guess my most faithful patron."

"Can't," Estelle said.

"Father Mouton's mother."

Estelle slowly absorbed the surprise. The corners of her mouth lifted in a tentative grin and that grin grew wider and wider until a deep long laugh exploded from her, so loud it sounded as if it had been buried inside her heart for years and years and soon the sun room echoed with rejoicing howls of laughter from both sisters.

"She wasn't really, was she?" Estelle wiped tears from her cheeks.

"Mrs. Mouton never missed her Thursday appointments. She put no more store into her son's warning than I did. 'Marie,' she said, 'I don't know what got into that boy. He always did come up with strange ideas. I tell you, I gave him a piece of my mind for trying to stir up a mess of foolishness.' I'm sure Father Mouton had good reason to regret that sermon."

The coffeepot was empty and the cookies gone by the time the sisters finished their visit. Ti-Rose was resting comfortably when Estelle lifted her for the trip home. "Her head feels a lot cooler," Estelle said.

Marie smiled. "I try to help. That's all I've ever tried to do."

Every day after that, Estelle returned to her sister's home. She and Marie spoke of many things, of years they had shared and of those they had not. On the fourteenth day, Marie died. Estelle wept for her sister's life, ended too soon, and she wept for herself.

Friends, clients, and relatives, including Estelle, flocked to Marie's funeral. Father Mouton was conveniently called out of town, so the funeral service was performed by a priest from the adjacent parish who could, with a straight face, pretend to know nothing of Marie's evil traiteuse ways and could, with a clear conscience, commend her soul to God.

letter to my older brother concerning the catholic church

You ask me why I am so angry about exclusion
and all-male priesthoods. Remember when
we were children, I helped you build
the tree house on the edge between field and woods;
yanked squealing nails from old planks,
lugged heavy two-by-fours, ignored splinters
from rough boards sawed the way you told me to?

When the platform was finished, you wouldn't let me in—
pushed me out until I went home wailing.
Oh, I could worship there when you were gone,
leaving my offerings spread out for the birds.
The sweetness of hay filled the air.
I loved the ribbed bark against my back,
suggestion of possibility in the endless sky.
But you always found me and I stomped away,
kicking at the innocent grass, confused
by my so-called sins against your sanctuary.

After a time, you went on to bigger trees
in the deep woods, where I wasn't allowed
because "things happened to little girls" there.
I got your hand-me-down house, hard-fought-for,
no victory came with it,
no quieting my hunger for unnamable things;
in this, too, I made do with what I was left.

I will
make do
no longer.

view from a tree

"Karin paces the floor, gesturing wildly as she talks. Heather, stretched out on the sofa, follows the erratic circles with her eyes, nodding from time to time at her partner's outbursts.

"It makes me furious. They're slaughtering the trees. They cut until there's nothing left. Those beautiful redwoods. They'll *never* grow back like that. And what can we do about it? Write more protest letters nobody reads?" At the end of the next arc, she slumps into a chair.

"Kim told me some people are going to Owl Valley," Heather says. "To try and stop the logging there."

"How?"

"Tree-sitters. Kim's going. And Leslie."

"You mean they're going to *climb* the trees? *Sit* in them? Those redwoods are two hundred feet tall!"

Heather nods. "They're doing a training. Tomorrow, I think."

Karin stares out the window at the wooded hills where treetops emerge from the mist. They are as magical as when she was a kid—the ones that are still left. Turning back to Heather, she asks, "Are you going?"

"I can't take time off work. Can you?"

"I've got a deadline." She looks out at the trees again. "Maybe I could write the story there."

"If you go, I'll do support when I can. I'll bake cookies to send up to your little platform."

Karin shudders. "Platform? You know I'm scared of heights. Even the orchard ladder."

Three nights later in the darkness of the forest, Karin stumbles down the steep slope with the other protesters. Each stump she trips on, each blackberry thorn that tears her flesh feels like a warning too late to heed. She wants to sing something courageous, all of them together at top volume. But North Lumber security guards might be scouting around.

They stop at the foot of a tree, throw down their gear. Looking up, Mark nods. "This one's good—no branches for eighty, ninety feet. I'll go up and rig it, then somebody can move in."

"Kim, I want a tree close to yours," Karin whispers, holding her friend's arm.

"Sorry," Mark says, "we've gotta spread out, cover the area. With only the three of you."

Karin watches him ascend the tree, straight up as though climbing the face of a cliff. Easy for him, she thinks, he's done it for years. Jack and the Beanstalk passing through the cloud—with the wicked giant waiting at the top. She reaches for Heather's hand.

One by one, Mark rigs the platforms. One by one, Kim and Leslie climb to theirs as Karin watches. And then they come to hers.

Nothing seems real except her fear. Trembling, she stands beneath the redwood, staring at the platform, suspended—from what? She looks beyond the platform to the branches above it, beyond the branches to the treetop, beyond the treetop to the sky. Pale light dilutes the darkness. Time to go. She turns, hugs Heather and Mark. He attaches the harness to her waist. "OK, you're secure. Go on up. We'll wait here."

With a deep breath, Karin puts her foot into the loop. "Focus on the rope...don't look down..." Mark's instructions march through her mind. "Raise the waist jumar...hang there on it...move the leg jumar up...stand on it..." Terror is only a glance, a thought away, but the task at hand takes total attention. Inches at a time, she moves up the rope.

The platform dangles above her head, one-by-twos bracing the thin plywood. How fragile it looks and still how far away. A deep breath. Another step up. Another. Another. She reaches her destination, pulls herself on. The platform shifts, swinging, with her weight. Her heart pounds. Sweat seeps from her cold forehead. On her knees, she clings to the board, clings to the lifeline, her hand frozen around the rope. Then she looks down, reeling with the height.

Heather waves, Mark calls. "Attach your carabiner clip to the safety line around the tree. Detach the jumars from your lifeline. Yeah. Now drop down the other end, and we'll tie on your supplies. Then we gotta get out of here. Call on the CB if you need anything."

"Or if you get lonely," Heather adds.

They wave good-bye and slip away through the trees, leaving her alone. A hundred feet above the ground.

She hauls up her pack of food and water and, with shaking hands, lashes it to the platform. Carefully, respectfully, she coils the rope and places it beside her, still clutching the end attached to the tree. This is her lifeline, her link to the ground, her way down whenever the time comes. Getting down—a thought more terrifying than staying here.

Anything else? She consults the checklist in her mind for tasks, to keep her fears at bay. The list completed, she considers her book or journal, the article she has to write. But stretching toward them sets the platform swinging. She recoils. What am I going to *do* up here? Can I handle the waiting? With a shiver she thinks, I don't even know what I'm waiting for.

The roar of chain saws answers her—muffled, some distance away. She tries to see where they are, but her view is screened by the other trees, and the direction disguised by the echo bouncing off the valley walls.

Exhausted from the long night's work, she unrolls her sleeping bag, but the end hangs over the edge of the platform. She curls up, but the space is hardly wide enough. What if the safety line comes unclipped or the lifeline slips out of her hand? What if she tosses in her sleep? The platform barely holds her lying still.

She faces the trunk of the tree that supports her. Huge, solid. It's been here for hundreds of years, she thinks, I should be able to count on it. Lacy branches fan out around the trunk. One brushes her head. Still gripping the rope, Karin reaches up with her other hand to touch the twig, running her fingers through its leaves as it runs its leaves through her hair. The touch gives her courage. So does the spicy evergreen smell—the same smell as the trees at home.

A wind comes up and rocks her bed, evoking the grim nursery tune which runs, uninvited, through her head. She edits the words and sings:

Rock-a-bye, baby, on the treetop,
when the wind blows the cradle will rock,
when the wind stops I'll take to the sky,
and that is the way I'll learn how to fly.

She sings it over and over until she falls asleep, held safe in the strength of the mother tree.

Voices from the ground hit Karin as she naps. She opens her eyes and sees the redwood trunk superimposed on a blur of green, reminding her where she is. Her lifeline is wrapped around her wrist, but she grabs it too, and grasping the platform, she turns. Peeking over the edge, she sees a handful of men, chain saws in hand, staring up at her. Now, even at this height, the tree feels safer than the ground. Unless they cut it down.

"Hey, baby, what you doin' up there?" One of the lumberjacks yells.

"Protecting this tree, to keep you from cutting it down," she answers, more defiantly than she feels.

"Be just as easy with you in it."

"More fun too," another laughs.

"Get down now if you got any sense. We're cutting our way over here, and it won't take long."

In her anger, Karin leans over. "No, it doesn't take you long. You destroy in a few hours these trees that took hundreds of years to grow."

"Look out, lady. You'll destroy yourself in minutes if you lean off your shelf. One nest egg. Scrambled."

The men leave, but the platform shakes with Karin's trembling. She takes out the CB. "This is Karin—in the tree."

"Hi," a staticky voice from base camp responds. "You OK?"

"I guess so. Is Heather there? Or Mark?"

"No. You need anything?"

A thousand things, she thinks—more space, hot coffee, an easy way down—but all she answers is, "A friend."

"You got one here, but you better sign off. Save your batteries for emergencies."

The voice is silent; she is alone again. She puts the CB away. Munches a handful of granola. Puts the granola away. She stares into the forest, searching the trees by the river. She longs for a glimpse of Kim or Leslie, but can't see either of them.

The woods, though, come to life. Green vibrates, brilliant on the young tips of the branches reaching out of last year's darker growth. Beside the water, alders shimmer where sun caresses their new leaves. A shower of twigs falls on her head, and she looks up to a jay hopping around on a higher branch. His raspy voice has courage in it, and Karin begins to sing. Peace songs, circle songs, folk songs. Love songs from years before. Mozart arias in a range she can't reach. Holly Near in a style she can't match.

The sky turns lavender and pink, then deepens into night. Karin closes her eyes, but remains wide awake. Unfamiliar noises rise from the ground—footsteps, the snapping of twigs. Raccoons? Deer? Or coyotes and bobcats? Maybe even mountain lions; they climb trees. Maybe men. They cut them down. Around her, owls call. She answers them with a low wail—a song of her own. And she gets through the night.

From her morning perch, Karin looks down at the sound of someone tramping through the woods. He's dressed in a brown plaid jacket and worn jeans, chain saw on his shoulder like a tool for his protection. Passing her platform, he stops and glares up. Karin holds tight to her rope and shouts, "When are you going to stop cutting these trees?"

"When we're done. When are you gonna get out of 'em?"

"When we know they're safe." Studying him, his slight stoop, his thick, grey hair, she adds, "You must think about them too. Have you been a logger for long?"

"All my life."

"They're making you cut awfully fast now. What will you do when the trees are gone?"

"There's still plenty around," he mumbles, then turns and leaves.

Sun touches the treetops on the hills. Between the branches, Karin watches the light expand and move along the ridge, then down the eastern-facing slope, painting the world green and golden. She smiles—eventually a transient spot of warmth will reach her. She nibbles some trail mix, drinks some water, brushes her teeth. Hanging onto the platform, she spits over the side and watches the globule fall—it seems so slowly—to the earth, where it disappears between the trillium and violet leaves.

The chain saws start, shattering the peace of the forest. They are louder today, coming closer. Then the terrible scream of a falling tree, taking the smaller ones with it as it crashes to the ground, shaking the earth, shaking her tree. Not a sound you could ever get used to, she thinks, the anguish a wave through her body. She tries to sing louder to drown it out, but the song won't come.

At noon, some of the loggers saunter over. "You still around?" one of them asks. "How does it look from there?"

"It looks horrible where you're cutting," she responds. "Empty. Sad."

"So don't look. Get down and go home."

"It'll grow back," adds the man in the brown plaid jacket.

"When? Not in our lifetime."

"Sure. America's renewable resource."

"Just like the company says," Karin's voice was shrill. "When are you going to stop listening to those North Lumber bosses and start listening to—"

"To you agitators?"

"No, listen to *yourselves*. The company doesn't care. They don't live here. They're in another state, another *world*. Some redwood paneled office—that's as close as they get to the trees you fell. They don't care about the trees, and they don't care about you."

"They're paying us, paying our jobs."

"How long will the jobs last, logging at this rate?" Karin asks.

"North Lumber owns this property. They can do what they want with it." He shrugs. "That's the system."

In the quiet of late afternoon when the men have left the woods, other voices speak to Karin in hums and chirps and crunches. Ravens call to each other and, perhaps, to her. A beetle arrives from somewhere, landing on her arm. It is blue and green and purple, iridescent, and tickles as it walks.

Karin takes a drink, feels the water slide down her throat. Tastes it. Realizes for the first time that water has a taste. The taste of the earth, of shade, the taste of a clear spring day.

Replacing the bottle, she notices her journal and picks it up to write: "Heather called on the CB. I don't know when—I don't even know how long I've been up here. Something has happened to time. Either it stopped or I'm someplace beyond it. There is day and there is night and everything is now.

"Nice to talk to Heather, hear her. The garden's growing, things are OK at home. Funny, it feels like I *am* home, like *this* is home. Like I'm one of the creatures of the woods, and we're all woven together. So I'm part of this tree, or she's part of me, and we both merge with the forest. There's some kind of force blending us all together—a powerful, sweet force…" The pen drops from her hand into the fold of the notebook beside a fragment of bark the tree has shed.

"Hey, you. Can you smell the coffee up there?" The loggers congregate to eat lunch and toss comments in her direction.

"My name's Karin."

"Hey Karin, come down and I'll give you coffee. I heard your friends over by the river are coming down. They're going home for the weekend. You going?"

Are they taunting her again, Karin wonders, or has something happened that base camp hasn't told her?

"You takin' the weekend off?" Now it's the grey-haired man with the brown plaid jacket who asks—the one they call Fred.

"No," she says. "I'm staying."

Through the windows between the branches, Karin watches the changing sky—shades of blue, shades of grey. In the wake of the sun, the ghostly light of a quarter moon silhouettes the hills, barren now where trees had been. Turning away, she burrows into her sleeping bag.

The roar of a generator breaks the silence, waking her with a jolt. Blinding searchlights invade the night, flashing through the trees. She pulls her cap down over her eyes, turns toward the shadow. The painful glare blazes around her—probing, attacking, violating.

At the base of the tree, a North Lumber guard shouts to be heard above the generator's racket. "You getting down now? We brought you some light to get down."

Karin closes her eyes and hangs onto the rope. Her fear comes back, but her anger has faded. She feels the intrusion, but it's part of something else—that man below is its agent and its victim. He's yelling again, but she doesn't hear his words. "Go away," she says, "please."

The searchlights withdraw, shifting toward the river, hunting the others. That will mean another day, another night before support can bring more supplies. She hasn't been eating much, but what she eats is dry food, and her water is almost gone.

Fog veils the region between night and day—damp, cold, wetting her face, seeping into her skin. She spreads her poncho over the sleeping bag and shrinks into a tighter ball, longing for the sun.

When the fog thins, she witnesses the desolation. They're cutting close, although her tree is still surrounded by others standing too near it to cut. Two other patches by the river indicate where Kim and Leslie are. As each tree falls, Karin feels the forest suffering. Still, she is with her tree; their destiny overlaps. And, mixed with sadness, she feels a healing force also present in these woods—a life force that will go on, knowing the way to go.

Now the voices on the ground are urgent, loud.

"Karin, you gotta come down and get outa here. We're gettin' close, and the foreman said to keep cutting."

She looks down at the men. "Who said we're more important than the trees? They don't take anything—they only give. But you're asking them to give too much when you take away their lives."

"Come on, we don't want you to get hurt."

"I'm part of this tree now, can't you see? If you take her, you'll have to take us both."

Fred lingers after the others have left. "I wish you'd come down now."

Karin shakes her head.

"Need anything?" he asks.

"Yes. I'm out of water."

"Throw your rope down. I'll send up my canteen."

She hesitates just for a moment, then lets down her lifeline.

She hangs in the sky like a cloud, each day more a part of the world around her. She touches the thick, spongy bark and puts her ear against the tree. Can she hear the sap moving through its capillaries like the blood that moves through hers? The platform doesn't seem far away now that her life is not only with the ground but also with everything above it. The osprey feeding her young. The hummingbird who visits her red sweater. The spider whose web spans the ropes that hold her platform. The morning mist that drifts around her, and the ray of sunlight that dissolves it, as she welcomes a new day.

threads of hope

We are the threads that bind us,
one to another: We strengthen
our babies' swaddling beginnings,
then loosen the ties so they can
wiggle in the wind like spring kites
soaring to new heights, finding
themselves: We are harmonious,
sturdy threads carefully woven
into the fiber of society,
where weak fabric frays: Some souls
fall through the holes into despair
and confusion and suffering.
We who are strong gather together
to tighten the knots and knit a net
of safety to catch those falling—
a shawl of comfort to dry their tears
and wrap their fears in courage.
We teach them to make their own shawls,
to become the threads that bind us,
one to another—with trust, with love.

the more things change

At ten o'clock on Tuesday morning when it is time to go see Irene, I am running my grocery store. Specifically, I am putting up a grocery order, stacking cans of tomato soup on the shelf. When I realize how late it is, I finish with the tomato soup and leave the chicken noodle on the floor, unpriced, still in the carton.

I had planned to change out of my dusty jeans and T-shirt into something more in keeping with the way Irene knew me in college. Perhaps something black and slinky with a turtleneck. But nowadays I don't do slinky. And I have no time to change. She'll see my true colors. Spilled coffee, orange soda, and price-gun ink. The colors of a grocer.

As I leave the store, I grab my purse, pen, and notebook. If it turns out Irene and I have nothing in common, at least I can write a story about her.

I call good-bye to my one employee who, if I am lucky, will put away the chicken noodle soup. I climb into my car and sit on the handle of the feather duster that is still stuck in my back pocket. I use it to dust the dashboard.

At the elementary school where Irene will perform, I park and find my way into the cafeteria. I sit next to the wall at a table where my knees bump the underside.

First, second, and third graders file in and sit on the floor in front of a stage. A boy tugs up his jeans that sag below the waistband of his turquoise boxer shorts. A girl wearing red hair ribbons stops in front of me. "Are you the Story Lady?" she asks.

"No," I answer. "I'm here to see her, too."

Irene and I have been out of touch for more than twenty years. Last week she saw my byline in the local paper, and telephoned to ask if I was the same Jean Blackmon she had known in college. I said I was. We agreed to meet today. Then I realized I am not the same person at all.

In college I was a writer and she was an actress. Together we marched for civil rights, protested Vietnam, pressed for women's liberation. Now I am occupied with groceries: tomatoes and lettuce, milk, eggs, and canned soup. She is known as the traveling Story Lady, and I am known for owning a grocery store.

Perhaps we have nothing in common.

In front of me the stage sparkles with color, a blue house, a green whale, purple birds, and two multicolored cardboard children. Recalling a survey that says older women carry bigger purses, I dig in my enormous bag for my pen and notebook. I take comfort in pens and notebooks.

Dressed in an indigo blouse and a long skirt of swirling colors, she steps onto the stage. I recognize her. Will she recognize me? We are both heavier. Our hair is lighter. Where once our faces were smooth now wrinkles have begun. Her eyes scan the audience and come to rest on me. I smile. She raises a hand in greeting, then begins.

"Parlez-vous Français?" She widens her eyes, spreads her arms, wiggles her hips. The children giggle at her wiggle and her exaggerated accent.

In a deeper voice, she says, "Buenos dias. Hablas Español?" She cups her hands behind her ears and waits for an answer.

A few children answer, "Si."

"Hi," she says. "Do you speak English?"

"Yes," the children shout. "Yes."

"Ahhh. A common language." She plants her hands on her hips and nods.

"I'm an actress who tells stories. And you are part of my stories. What shall we use to tell our stories?"

"Words," says the girl wearing red hair ribbons.

"Good," Irene says. "We'll use words. Let's also use our bodies." She twists and crouches, then leaps to her full height. The children laugh. "And we'll use our voices." She warbles, growls, yodels. Again they laugh.

My mind reaches back more than twenty years to a dorm room.

"Test me," Irene had said. "Give me an acting problem."

"Be a fried egg," I said, thinking I had asked the impossible.

She cracked her rigid shell over the back of a chair and slithered onto the floor. Her body twitched, as if frying in hot oil. With her tongue she made popping sounds.

Now I watch her on stage. Strutting. Twirling. Telling stories. The characters she portrays ask questions. Who is more important, the king or the queen? Which is more beautiful, black or white? Usually her words are English. Sometimes they are French. Sometimes Spanish. Though the children don't understand every word, they understand her body language. That is where she is most fluent. Some things don't change.

I scribble notes, sort through words to describe her.

When she finishes, she introduces me as her friend, her classmate, as these children are classmates.

"Jean is a writer," she says. "See how she takes notes. She always took notes. A writer."

I want to correct her, to tell her I run a grocery store. Instead, I raise my hand, the hand that holds my pen, and wave to the children.

Over a sea of small faces, we smile.

fertility goddess

Morning glories unfold
when she sings at dawn.
By afternoon, tomatoes swell
and the first apples redden.

Sunset tucks her beneath
silver artichoke arms,
the flowering cape
of a strawberry bed.

All night she dreams of
zucchini and eggplant,
strokes warm dirt like
a quilt's satin binding.

She smiles and sighs
in her sleep.
Secret carrots stretch
and juicy radishes fatten.

In the selective stockpile
of past harvest and bloomings,
she composts grey mistakes which
December has weeded.

delivery

You start in the shallows,
pains too far apart to pant;
your paddle dips and sculls
out of the rippled rocks.
Then you come to a small chute
of standing waves,
the patterns sing and dance.
You breathe, stroke,
ride high on each crest,
rest in the trough.
Transition comes: the water
breaks, a tricky Class III.
The rocks are random,
the way is hard to spot,
but you don't swamp
or give in to pain:
around the bend
just one chute more
to the takeout place.
The rocks are huge,
the path unclear,
but one last push
and you'll be through.
You blow and blow,
sliding past the whirlpool,
the sheer steep cliffs
into the calm flat water.
The baby cries, her sound
sparkling like a million mornings;
the moving river goes on.

on viewing judy chicago's birth project: four needlepoint paintings

One:
The trinity of female bodies birth and flow
  forms of endurance curve powerful hands to create
   curve rays of sun to light the earth of women
    curve love of self flowing to me
the moon blinds the forces of darkness the horsemen wait

Two:
The power lights her body her hands hold pulsing legs
  in birth push and orgasm the oval pelvis contracts
   as she shouts the triumphant birthing cry
    hair flying in rays of light rebirthing the world
with fire holding at bay the thunderous horsemen

Three:
Another woman sad and dark births and suckles
  the world's ravenous need for bodies her babies
   are war machines and her endurance invaded without end
    hunger and despair diminish her in moon dark
the horsemen husband and control her power

Four:
Unveil the light Power of Unknown One reveal the body
  of the moon woman who flows to barren rock who touches
   stars and blooms in dinosaurs and fish and flowers
    who reveals the parting of seas and birthing of babies
to create the cherishing of mother earth

We the viewers of the birth project lean our women bodies
  closer entranced each stitch and needlepoint done by
   women of the world perfect and intimate we step back
    to see celebration of breasts and thighs
power and life it is the birthing of women and we cry.

the long night

Sally Conlon napped sitting up, a soft snuffling noise keeping the rhythm of her breath. In her hands, a paperback novel lay open, the pages hugging her belly. Coffee cooled in a mug on the pine table beside the couch.

She dreamed. In the scene behind her papery eyelids, a younger Sally walked barefoot across the muddy flats of a retreating lake bed. Fiery orange light glowed through trees that looked cut from construction paper. Clouds passed over a full moon peeking through the trees. In the dream Sally felt as though she were walking through a Halloween collage she'd made in grade school. She was looking for someone but couldn't have said exactly who or why.

She woke to real, wind-driven rain pelting her living room window. The old woman lay with her eyes closed for a few minutes trying to hold to the sense of the dream. She didn't try to decipher the meaning of her dreams anymore, deep or otherwise; instead she savored the feelings left by them. This morning's left a curious impression of calm anticipation.

Sally treasured her catnaps for their very nearness to her dream memories, viewing her reveries as well-earned gifts of her later years. She chuckled thinking how ridiculously easy to entertain she had become.

She no longer slept the sweet uninterrupted seven or eight hours taken as normal by people younger than herself, but took her sleep in abbreviated sessions and tried to put a good face on all the extra time she had. This morning, she had padded out to the kitchen at twenty past four to make her first coffee.

At eighty-five, she didn't cover a lot of ground most days. She still drove, often heading for the twenty-four-hour grocery before the streets were full of drivers on a schedule tighter than her own. It wasn't the easiest time to shop what with the aisles full of cartons and those young stockers uniformly decked out in Walkmans moving to a beat kept from her ears. A few of them had gotten to know her; they'd ask how she was doing and help with the reaching.

In the predawn she'd imagine herself the lead character in a spy novel. Or a lady cop tailing desperate criminals. Innocent amusement in a life that had otherwise slowed in the most natural way. Not wanting to be judged bonkers and railroaded into some home, she kept her fantasies to herself.

She remembered how, as a young woman, she'd been grateful to her parents for giving her a name that would carry her gracefully into old age. Sarah Elizabeth. Only thing was, she had never made the change from Sally to Sarah, not with her friends or in her heart.

Now she straightened up on the couch, rose slowly and walked to the window. The day would have been dreary had it not been such an odd December storm. Wind was slanting a drenching rain nearly sideways across her view and thunder rumbled miles away. She felt bad for the folks who were out finishing the last of their Christmas shopping.

Sally's holiday chores were done. Her gift and card list had grown shorter each year. She'd been married for a short time in her thirties but it hadn't been a good idea and there had been no children and so, of course, no grandchildren. None of those photos with four and five generations graced her mantel. Her brothers were both gone. There were nieces and nephews and their children, mostly back East. Their holiday cards stood displayed on the window sill. Sally would be driven to Albuquerque in a few days to eat Christmas ham with Steven and his wife, the only ones living nearby.

Years ago, an astrologer had told her that a person ought to live to eighty-four in order to complete all the cycles of life. That might be so. What the astrologer had neglected to add was that a complete life would be solitary toward the end. One by one, Sally had outlived her closest friends.

They used to laugh about living together in their dotage, she and Sandra and Bonnie. They would wear what they liked and eat when they felt like it and not care that anyone thought them odd. They had never lived together after all, but had stayed dear to one another right to the finish. Sandra had been gone for many years now and Bonnie, not quite two.

Scenes of their times together passed before Sally's eyes as she stood at the window, the images not unlike the film-clip sequences in her dreams. They'd had great adventures, some of them well orchestrated, others unplanned like the time she and Bonnie were caught trespassing so far up in the hills or when the three of them, keen to see one more mile of forest-service road, knocked the oil pan off Sandra's car.

They had seen one another through heartbreaks and triumphs, mind-numbing jobs, loves, and everyday calls to strength and humor. Sandra's only child had been as near a daughter as Sally was ever to have. One had finished sentences for the other and understood things that couldn't be framed in words. They had reveled in the richness of being and the gift of their womanhood.

The wind outside was easing and rain changed to huge swirling flakes as though some force high overhead had realized the inappropriateness of rain in this season and turned a dial to the proper weather. Sally watched the flakes melt into the soggy ground, then gain mass and begin to cover her yard in downy softness.

She turned from the window and made her way carefully to the kitchen, putting on tea water and dropping an English muffin into the toaster. She leaned against the counter and checked a calendar hung beside the stove. Why, it's Solstice, she thought. Winter begins.

She thought again of Bonnie and Sandra and the first time they lit a bonfire to mark the long night. It must have been more than forty years ago. From that time forward they had declared the Solstice their personal New Year.

The first fire had been Sally's idea. Of the three, Sally had struggled

most with the darkness of winter, the daylight cut short by a low traveling sun. She had learned to cheer her flagging spirit by counting the
days before Solstice; calculating, for instance, that if the day were only
two weeks away, then this was the worst four weeks and she could surely
tolerate another four weeks. She would note sunrise and sunset times,
thankful for every minute gained on the journey toward spring.

She buttered the muffin generously, heedless of an unfashionable girth
or clogged veins. She ate so little anymore that neither were a cause for
concern. Another joke of her advancing years: now when she could have
cared less, her extra enemy ten pounds had retreated beyond some
unseen border.

She ate slowly and wondered when the bonfires had stopped. Ice and
cold and unsteady legs must have brought caution some years back.
And Sally had made peace with the dark as sleep had fallen away and
more and more of her reading was done through the hushed hours of
the night.

She sat for a long time with the tea, watching the snow pile on to bare
tree limbs and tussocks of grass in her back yard. It would take some
planning, she thought, but what didn't at this age? I'll have to find those
old hiking boots and layer myself into lots of warm things. And the fire
itself; I'll need some way to get it started out there.

The old woman realized she was excited. It wasn't often anymore that
she felt excitement; mostly she felt at peace, accepting of her own wind-
ing down.

She spent the hours until dark much as she would any afternoon, reading two more chapters of the paperback and working for a bit on an
afghan she was knitting for Steve's family. Periodically she would rise
and gather up clothing or newspaper for the coming ceremony. She got
a cane from the closet and set it out by the back door. Ordinarily, she
would have catnapped once or twice but a quiet hum of expectancy
made sleep unnecessary.

At ten minutes past six, Sally began pulling on long johns and sweatpants, two pairs of socks and a good heavy sweater. She sat on the edge of her bed, willing herself to take her time, resisting a tug of urgency. The boots were stiff with sitting on a shelf, unneeded for so long. Finally she stood, wrapping a scarf over a woolly tam and pulling on her coat, stuffing gloves into the pockets.

At the back door, she took the cane in one hand and in the other, a shopping bag she had stocked that afternoon. The bag held newspaper knots and a box of farmer's matches. She pushed the door open to a covered patio and laid the bag on a lawn chair, then dragged the whole lot into the yard. Her steps were short and steadied by the cane.

Returning to the patio, she gathered a small armful of kindling and made her way back to the lawn chair. Steven had cut the kindling three winters ago, but it had sat unused; up to now she hadn't seen the sense of messing with a fire. Back and forth she went until she was satisfied there was enough fuel.

Using the cane as a balance, a sort of tripod leg, she laid the paper knots in a pile on the snow and stood small sticks of wood in a teepee around the paper. She added a few larger pieces of the pine. She took her time, placing the wood with care and checking her balance with every bend toward the earth. Her breath sent tiny clouds of steam drifting through the sharp air.

She straightened and, holding to the chair back, surveyed her work. Yes, she thought, her modest effort world do nicely for seeing out the year without rousing the fire department. She lowered herself into the lawn chair and eased herself to the edge, then bent once more toward the ground, this time putting a match to one of the paper knots. She sat back and watched as tongues of blue-green flame danced in the pine.

It was done. She had brought light to the longest night. She closed her eyes and saw for a moment the others, Bonnie and Sandra, standing on the other side of the flames, bundled like herself, laughing.

in praise of spinsters

I am no castoff
no raggedy
I am as bountiful as corn
my face turned toward the sun
I sing in praise of spinsters
who weave their hair
to make strong rope
who cast their dreams
to make fine pots
We are your mystery
the ones who slipped away
I celebrate what we are—
clay sifting through fingers—
women alone
harvesting the earth

Photo by Gwynyth Lozier Milsin

winter solstice

i stand on the moon, my shadow reflected in its pale light. on the planet below women everywhere are dancing and bathing, drawing colors on each other's breasts. it's my party, i smile, a time for magic and moon-light. i quietly descend to one of the celebrations. in a small island village i find twenty-five women of all ages and sizes, gathered around a hot pool. the weather is far from tropical, this is canada after all. no snow, just cool rain and tall cedar trees—a paradise of eagles and mountains all looking to the sea.

breasts sag on many of these women, and the marks of childbirth are drawn on their bellies and legs. wrinkles line some of their faces and crow's-feet splay from the corners of their eyes. they have lived some years and look content in their way, their faces shining in the firelight as they hold each others' hands and hips, swaying to the music.

one woman, she tells me her name is rose, welcomes me to the circle. my place is set with candles and pine boughs, and she fills my hand with rose petals as i pass through the archway. i face a goddess of red paint and charcoal drawn upon the wall. i smile at the likeness of myself and long for the ample bosom of the woman they've adorned. lately full-bodied goddesses are again in high esteem.

we begin the ceremony, pass the talking stick, and chant one song after another as our candles flicker in the breeze. we bring in the new light and let go of the darkness for another year, talking of the shadowy time. i listen as some women extol it, while others admit their fear of the night wind and winter storms.

i'm surprised to hear so many speak fondly of the dark, of its calm, the soft cave it forms around them. i for one hate the winter and am always glad when the cycle turns again. it's tedious to be groping about with candles, carrying an umbrella, and doing all my celestial chores with so little light in each day. but here the women, some mothers, some crones, a few women-lovers i think, try to embrace each season equitably, a cyclical civil rights of sorts. i listen and enjoy the mulled wine.

the drumming begins again and the women rise to dance. music moves their hips as they reach to the sky, naked and beginning to sweat. circling each other they wail as the beat grows faster. on the moonlit deck they move together until the drummers tire, then feast and drink until the early hours of the morning. these women fete as if each moment were their last. i ask one of them how this celebration began.

"twice a year we delight ourselves, at summer and winter solstice. many women are away from their men and their children tonight, from all the parts of their lives that tie them to their homes. the drumbeat reminds them of all they long for between these celebrations. passion, freedom to howl at the moon, these are the things they have given up to be with men. they hide this part of themselves in order to live their lives." her partner sits across the room, smiling at us. both their faces are lined, and she tells me their children are grown and gone.

the evening ends and i leave quietly, thanking my hostesses for the beautiful rites. i walk along their country road, past log cabins and pick-up trucks, down a path to a deserted beach. here the ocean hisses through gleaming stones, bequeathing tree trunks and centuries of water in quiet eddies and colossal waves. the ocean is my refuge. here i'm reminded of my efforts, of what remains of the planet i watch over. she is the reflection of my mourning and the music of my solitude. i sit with her and listen.

clouds blow past the stars and across the moon; i lift myself on the wings of the wind and pass over houses and gardens to begin another year. the celebrations of women fill me with their longing. in my hand are the words of the crone next to me at the solstice circle. she'd thrown the paper into the fire but i rescued it. here is what she wrote.

power is…
seeing the wrinkles in my face and laughing
feeling the hill beneath my feet and the river in my face
staying behind to be alone
reading a book on new year's eve
loving time as it passes
mourning all i don't know
learning that learning is the most exciting thing left
wishing the chatter of my mind would stop
being opinionated without apology
observing i will not change much now
laughing when some don't like me, but not really caring much
having more people in my life than i have inclination to see
realizing we aren't all meant to like each other, just learn to disagree

power is…
noticing i can only change the present and the future; the past is gone.
believing that peace and sex into my nineties are totally possible.

in place

In solitude, you become nocturnal,
sleep in the afternoon, wake at dusk,
and step into the clearing then.
The day will stay as it is,
but the night bears watching.

Perhaps you are essential.
Without you, the sky would sprawl and spread
over the meadow, like seawater.
Stars would glitter in the grass;
you would have to toss them back, one by one,
as though they were gasping silver fish.

Keeping the universe in place
takes all your strength.
Imagine it is not empty, but everywhere.
Imagine it is not heavy, but so light
that it must be tethered
to the thread of your chimney smoke
to keep it from drifting off.
Imagine your loneliness is not swallowing you,
only bathing you with its wide wet tongue.

Before you lose yourself, choose and touch
points of reference: the cabin door, the Douglas fir
with its naked trunk, the corner post of the outhouse,
the twisted cedar on the edge of the bluff.

Then stir the cauldron of stars with your reaching hand.
Ladle star soup in your cupped palm, and drink it.

Or imagine the sky is studded with sharp points
like thumbtacks you can press into patterns and rearrange.

If you give a name to any constellation,
it will follow you, day and night,
looking over your shoulder.
If you find a place for yourself,
you will still circle the bowl of your isolation.

You will have to give your heart
back to the water,
watch it flick away from your hand,
to join a school of silver fish,
whirled in a vortex, or suspended
in a net of branches.

time out of mind

Where there are many witnesses,
A tribe is born.
We sit around the circle,
Listening to each other's
Stories in our skins.

In the morning, the deep
Glow of fire against the
Cave wall tells us:
It is another time.
Out of our mouths come
Petroglyphs that attach
Themselves to the cave
Walls, to be admired by
Ourselves now, & pondered by
Archaeologists in days to come.

We started with a laugh—
And end with a cackle.
Something has changed after
Round after round after round:
Our teeth are sharper & more
Pronounced, our hair wilder,
The right breast missing,
To more easily draw the bow.

acknowledgments

Grateful acknowledgment is made to the following publications which first published some of the material in this book:

Corrales Comment, August 6, 1994, for "The More Things Change" by Jean Blackmon; *Womanpriest: A Personal Odyssey* (LuraMedia, 1988), *Stars in Your Bones: Emerging Signposts on Our Spiritual Journeys* (North Star Press, 1990), *Gynergy* (Wisdom House, 1978), *Water Women* (Wisdom House, 1990), and *All Shall Be Well/All Shall Be One* (Wisdom House, 1991), for "Call" by Alla Renée Bozarth; *Fighting Woman News,* Vol. 19, No. 4, #51, Fall 1993 for "The Glass-Smashing Wall" by Pam Burris; *Many Mountains Moving,* Winter 1995, Volume 2, No. 1 for "The Dancing Girl's Story" by May-Lee Chai; *Sgraffito Press,* Issue #3, Fall 1996/Winter 1997 for "A Fable of Obeah Women" by Dominique Chlup; *Bloodroot,* 1978 for "Delivery" by Barbara Crooker; *The Celibacy Club* (City Lights, 1997) for "Gypsy Lore" in a slightly different form by Janice Eidus; *Sing Heavenly Muse,* Anniversary Issue, No. 17, 1990, for "She Pours" in a slightly different form by Blanche Flanders Farley; *The Panhandler,* Issue 24, 1992, for "The Traiteuse" by Jacqueline Guidry; *Full Circle Eighteen* (Guild Press, 1997) for "Black Woman" by Cynthia Hatten; *Liberty Hill Poetry Review,* Issue No. 2, Spring 1995 for "Fertility Goddess" by Jennifer Lagier; *Earth's Daughters,* No. 42, © 1994 for "New Politics in Salem" by Joanne McCarthy; The Julian Center of Indianapolis, 20th Anniversary, 1995, and *The Village Sampler,* May 1995 and April 1997, for "Threads of Hope" by Shirley Vogler Meister; Matrix 35 and *The Work of Our Hands* (The Muses' Company, 1992) for "Silencing" by Sharon H. Nelson; *American Poetry Anthology,* Volume X, No. 2 for "My Ambivalence" by Estelle Padawer; *Mendocino Beacon,* September 14, 1995, for "Hard Times for Women" by Fionna Perkins; *VERVE Magazine* for "Woman's Work" by Diane Reichick; *Wake Up and Smell the Coffee, Chicken Soup for the Soul: A Second Helping,* and *Chicken Soup for the Teenage Soul* for "After a While" © 1971 by Veronica A. Shoffstall; *Poet & Critic,* Spring 1989, Volume 20, No. 3 for "The Women Who Married" by Donna Spector; *The Mendonesian,* August 1996, and *Saltwater, Sweetwater* (Floreant Press, 1997) for "View from a Tree," by Sunlight; and *The Bridge,* Spring 1994 for "Tough" by Edwina Trentham.

contributors

DORI APPEL is an award-winning poet, playwright, and fiction writer, whose work has appeared in five previous Papier-Mache anthologies. Of her twelve produced plays, *Girl Talk,* coauthored with Carolyn Myers, was published (Samuel French, 1992) and "Friendship," a monologue from *Female Troubles,* is included in *More Monologues by Women, for Women* (Heinemann, 1996). *p. 135*

KIRSTEN BACKSTROM writes poetry, fiction, and essays. Her work has appeared in *The Georgia Review, Arkansas Review, The American Voice,* and other journals, as well as in the Papier-Mache anthology, *If I Had My Life to Live Over I Would Pick More Daisies.* She lives in Portland, Oregon. *p. 178*

MIRIAM BASSUK recently moved to Mill Creek, Washington, where she is marking her midlife transition by writing letters and poetry and taking classes. Her poems have been published in The Journal of Sacred Feminine Wisdom, *Writers' Wings,* and The Person-Centered Journal. *p. 21*

THERESE BECKER's poetry, photography, essays, and journalism have appeared in numerous magazines, newspapers, and anthologies, including *Full Court: A Literary Anthology of Basketball, DoubleTake,* and *Poetry East.* She has a masters in creative writing from Warren Wilson College and teaches the creative process through the Michigan Council for the Arts, Creative Writers in the Schools program. Her new book, *Good Medicine,* will enumerate successful creative process exercises. *p. 51*

JEAN BLACKMON is a columnist, short story writer, and essayist. Her work appears in books, newspapers, and magazines, including two previous Papier-Mache anthologies. She and her husband, John Waszak, live in Corrales, New Mexico, where they own the Frontier Mart, a mom and pop grocery store. *p. 162*

LAUREL ANN BOGEN is the author of eight collections of poetry and short fiction. She teaches poetry and performance in the UCLA Extension Writer's Program and is poetry director of the Arundel Poetry Series. Afflicted with the poetry obsession early in life—she won an Academy of American Poets college award as a freshman at USC in 1968—there is still no abatement. *p. 173*

THE REV. DR. ALLA RENÉE BOZARTH is one of the Philadelphia Eleven, the first women ordained Episcopal priests in 1974, a saga she describes in her autobiographical book, *Womanpriest: A Personal Odyssey.* Her poetry is widely anthologized. She is the author of eight prose books and nine poetry collections as well as five audiotapes. She practices priesthood and soul care work as a contemplative artist at Wisdom House in Sandy, Oregon. *p. 8*

JODY LANNEN BRADY is a freelance writer, with publications in numerous magazines, newspapers, and journals. She writes fiction with the generous support of her writing group. She lives in Annandale, Virginia, with her husband, Bill, and her children, Matt and Kelly. *p. 45*

PAM BURRIS, born and educated in southern California, is an administrator at the State University of New York, Stony Brook. She has previously published in literary magazines and is currently working on a novel based on her story, "The Glass-Smashing Wall." *p. 99*

MAY-LEE CHAI is the author of a novel, *My Lucky Face* (Soho Press), set in Nanjing, China. Her short stories have appeared in many journals, including the *Missouri Review, North American Review,* and *Seventeen.* She is currently at work on a second novel. *p. 36*

DOMINIQUE CHLUP, originally from Jamaica, teaches learning disabled students in New York City. She received her MFA from Sarah Lawrence. Previous works have appeared in *Oval Magazine, Columbia Review,* and *Buffalo Bones.* She won a 1996 Writer's Digest Award and just completed writing a novel. *p. 120*

JAMIE COPE has printed and exhibited her portraits and documentaries for twenty-five years. She has received honors and grants from the Gulbenkian Foundation, Lisbon, and Le Mussé d'Art Moderne de la Ville de Paris, Paris; The Polaroid Foundation; Honeywell, Inc.; the NEA; and others. She now resides in Montpelier, Vermont. *p. 159*

MARIL CRABTREE is a writer, environmental educator, and mediator. She shares community life with several others in a "recycled" house in Kansas City's urban core and believes sustainable relationships are a key factor in creating a more sustainable world. *p. 126*

BARBARA CROOKER has published six hundred poems in magazines and anthologies, including *Worlds in Their Words: Contemporary American Writers* (Prentice Hall) and *A Whole Other Ballgame: Women Writing Women's Sports* (Farrar, Straus & Giroux). "Delivery" was written to celebrate the birth of her daughter who, at eighteen, suffered a traumatic brain injury and was in a coma for ten days, but who miraculously recovered and is now in college as an honors engineering student. *p. 166*

BETTY DAVIS a freelance writer for many years, lives in Houston, Texas. A member of the Austin Writer's League, her fiction and poetry have been most recently seen in *Maverick Press, Second Glance, Poems That Jump in the Dark, Just Write, Lilliput, Dream Machinery, Patchwork Poems,* and three anthologies. She has also published a poetry chapbook, *Clues* (Chili Verde Press). *p. 71*

JANICE EIDUS, twice winner of the prestigious O. Henry Prize for her short stories, as well as a Pushcart Prize, is the author of two short story collections, *The Celibacy Club* and *Vito Loves Geraldine,* and two novels, *Urban Bliss* and *Faithful Rebecca.* She is also coeditor of the forthcoming anthology, *It's Only Rock 'n' Roll: Rock 'n' Roll Short Stories.* Her work has been widely published in anthologies and magazines in the U.S. and abroad. *p. 26*

KAREN ETHELSDATTAR's poems and liturgies, including interfaith celebrations, affirm women and the feminine presence of God. She is cofounder of a women's ritual group, Eve's Well. Her poems have appeared in *Woman Spirit; Off Our Backs, New Women, New Church;* and in Starhawk's *The Spiral Dance.* Her name is taken to honor her mother. *p. 22*

BLANCHE FLANDERS FARLEY, a librarian in Atlanta, Georgia, is coeditor of *Like a Summer Peach: Sunbright Poems and Old Southern Recipes* (Papier-Mache Press, 1996). A group of her poems, "Grave Numbers," set to music by Clare Shore for soprano and guitar, was performed last year at The National Museum of Women in the Arts. *p. 74*

MARY GERKEN considers herself an environmentalist and feminist, both of which have shaped her poetry. She works for the Environmental Protection Agency and does creation awareness and gay/lesbian outreach ministries for her church, while trying to keep her sense of humor. *p. 137*

JANE GLEESON's award-winning photos and articles have been published in numerous magazines. She has taught both photography and nursing at the college level. Her background in health often influences her writing. She works with the camera in a documentary style. *p. 82*

JENNY GOLDBERG, a photographer and writer, lives in Taos, New Mexico. Her carpentry class (a bunch of men and two women) built a shed. She decided to focus on the art in hand and not take pictures, but when Sally Torres started hammering the rafters, she couldn't resist. *p. 117*

JACQUELINE GUIDRY writes fiction and personal essays. Besides writing, she practices law part-time, specializing in Social Security disability benefits; volunteers as a fiction editor for *Potpourri;* and tries to keep up (often unsuccessfully) with two teenage daughters. *p. 138*

ROSE HAMILTON-GOTTLIEB's fiction has appeared in *Aethlon, Room of One's Own, The Elephant Ear, Farm Wives and Other Iowa Stories, Prairie Hearts: Women Writing on the Midwest,* and *Grow Old Along with Me—The Best Is Yet to Be. p. 86*

CYNTHIA HATTEN was born in Cleveland, Ohio, and now resides in Plainsboro, New Jersey. Her poems and short stories have appeared in *African Voices,* Guild Press anthologies, and other publications. She is currently working on a novel, and she enjoys silk painting, flower arranging, and aromatherapy. *p. 43*

KAREN J. HOKE's love for creative writing was nurtured at Manchester Community College. She graduated from St. Joseph College for Women and is doing graduate studies at the University of Hartford, where she also works as a grant writer. She lives in Manchester, Connecticut, with her children, Rob, Kylie, and Andy. *p. 25*

HONORÉE FANONNE JEFFERS, a Rona Jaffe Foundation for Women Writers awardee, holds an MFA from the University of Alabama. Her work has appeared in several journals and anthologies, including *African American Review, Dark Eros,* and *Crab Orchard Review. p. 85*

MARY KELLY, now forty-seven, has lived in northern New Mexico for over twenty years and has worked most of those years in the fine art foundry business. She has often sat with her women friends, wrapped in a blanket, eating hot dogs around a December bonfire. *p. 168*

JAN KEMPSTER has been a river guide in Arizona and Idaho since 1984. She recently completed building a dory, the Animas, which she rows in the Grand Canyon. She has an MA in English from Northern Arizona University, and has lived in Flagstaff for nine years. She currently works as a librarian in a school on the Navajo Reservation. *p. 53*

CARRIE KNOWLES, author of *Alzheimer's: The Last Childhood* (Research Triangle Publishing), understands both the power and the problems of being a caretaker. Married with three children, she writes fiction and nonfiction but is a poet at heart. *p. 97*

WILLA KORETZ, founder of Santa Fe's *Out on a Limb!* Poetry Series, broke out of Harvard's Young Poets Program in 1971 to go the unconventional route: writing international image-making copy by day and composing the poetry she loves (now much anthologized) by night. *p. 180*

MARY JACKSON KRAUTER lives with her husband and three children in Bridgeport, Nebraska. Encouraged by her mother, she began writing in her midthirties and has recently returned to college. She published a chapbook, *Clippings* (Pudding House Publications, 1995), and has also been published by *California Sate Poetry Quarterly,* the University of Iowa, and *Emerging Voices. p. 107*

JENNIFER LAGIER, cochair of the National Writers Union, Local 7, has published in *When I Am an Old Woman I Shall Wear Purple, If I Had My Life to Live Over I Would Pick More Daisies, Unsettling America: An Anthology of Contemporary Multicultural Poetry,* and *Voices in Italian Americana. p. 165*

JANICE LEVY is the author of *The Spirit of Tío Fernando, Adventures of Filimina, Abuelito Goes Home, Totally Uncool,* and *Abuelito Eats with His Fingers.* Her adult fiction has appeared in *If I Had My Life to Live Over I Would Pick More Daisies* and *Glimmer Train. p. 9*

JUDY LIGHTWATER is a lesbian feminist novelist and activist. She lives in Victoria, British Columbia, Canada, where she walks on the beach every day while talking to herself. Her two grandchildren, Max and Madison, remind her to view the world with wonder. *p. 175*

KATHRYN HOWD MACHAN loves, writes, dances, and teaches near one of the Finger Lakes of Central New York. She is a member of the Writing Program faculty of Ithaca College and of Mirage: Ithaca's Belly Dancers. Her "Wise Woman" poem in this collection celebrates her best friend, Rosalie Manzi, with whom she has shared dreams and deeds for well over three decades. *p. 7*

JOANNE MCCARTHY has cut short her life as a teacher in order to concentrate on her life as a writer. Her poems appear in numerous anthologies and journals, most recently *Claiming the Spirit Within* (Beacon Press, 1996), *Calyx, Kalliope,* and *Writers' Forum.* She believes that women can do anything they want. *p. 68*

SHIRLEY VOGLER MEISTER is an award-winning Indianapolis freelancer with prose and poetry in diverse U.S. and Canadian publications. Her poetry—in print more than four hundred times—is included in five other Papier-Mache anthologies: *When I Am an Old Woman I Shall Wear Purple, If I Had My Life to Live Over I Would Pick More Daisies, I Am Becoming the Woman I've Wanted, Grow Old Along with Me—The Best Is Yet to Be,* and *There's No Place Like Home for the Holidays. p. 160*

GWYNYTH LOZIER MISLIN celebrated and mourned the end of summer 1996 with Mary Christie and their community of friends and neighbors at their beloved and venerable Olentangy Village Pool, built in 1899. In Mary's face, she found the courage to brave the winter ahead. *p. 174*

LILIAN NATTEL has fun teaching creative writing to senior citizens in Toronto, Canada. An excerpt from her forthcoming novel about women and life in a Polish shtetl, *The River Midnight,* appears in *Sweet Secrets: Stories of Menstruation* (Second Story Press, 1997). *p. 77*

DIEDRE NEILEN, PhD, is an associate professor of humanities at the SUNY Health Science Center in Syracuse, New York. When not writing fiction, she teaches creative writing, film, and literature to students in the health care professions, nursing, and medicine. *p. 128*

SHARON H. NELSON's poems often focus on how the lives of girls and women are constructed. Her books include *Mad Women and Crazy Ladies, Grasping Men's Metaphors,* and *Family Scandals.* She writes and edits poetry and nonfiction in Montreal. *p. 1*

MARILYN NOLT, a resident of Souderton, Pennsylvania, has been providing photo illustrations for periodicals, books, brochures, and calendars for nearly twenty years. Her files include candid images of children and adults as well as landscapes and stills. *pp. 24, 70, 76, 136, and 161*

KEDDY ANN OUTLAW lives and writes in Houston, Texas. She is a librarian and edits *Arrowsmith* magazine. Her poems, stories, and book reviews have appeared in *Borderlands: Texas Poetry Review, Grasslands Review, Lilliput Review, Exit 13, Kumquat Meringue, i.e. magazine, Library Journal, the Houston Chronicle,* and *I Am Becoming the Woman I've Wanted* (Papier-Mache Press). She was selected as a juried poet in the 1989 and 1994 Houston Poetry Fests. *p. 118*

ESTELLE PADAWER, a former educator and cost analyst, living in Fort Lee, New Jersey, directs her creative energies to writing poetry and designing note cards. Her poem in this anthology, "My Ambivalence," won an award in a nationwide contest. Others mostly appear in small magazines. *p. 72*

NITA PENFOLD is a poet, an artist, a director of religious education, and a grandmother. She has published several short stories and over two hundred poems in the past sixteen years since she discovered her voice and her power were the same. *p. 147*

FIONNA PERKINS, the granddaughter of a suffragist, has been a newspaperwoman and political activist. Her poetry was first published in the mid-thirties. Her fiction and poetry has appeared in several anthologies, including *When I Am an Old Woman I Shall Wear Purple, Cartwheels on the Faultline,* and *Saltwater, Sweetwater* (Floreant Press). She lives on the Mendocino coast of California. *p. 83*

ANDREA POTOS lives in Madison, Wisconsin, with her husband and daughter. Her poems recently appeared in *Calyx* and *Claiming the Spirit Within: A Sourcebook of Women's Poetry* (Beacon Press). *p. 5*

MARGARET RANDALL is a poet, essayist, oral historian, and photographer, whose most recent titles include *The Price You Pay: The Hidden Cost of Women's Relationship to Money* (Routledge) and *Hunger's Table: Women, Food & Politics* (Papier-Mache Press). Her photographs have been exhibited in Mexico, Venezuela, Nicaragua, Canada, and the United States. *pp. xxii, 6, 44, 52, 84, and 108*

DIANE REICHICK is the founding editor of *VERVE Magazine*. She is also vice president of the National League of American Pen Women, Simi Valley Branch, and received its 1994–96 Woman of Achievement Award. She directs the Dorothy Daniels Annual Writing Contest. *p. 66*

ELISAVIETTA RITCHIE's *Flying Time: Stories and Half-Stories* contains four PEN Syndicated Fiction winners. Her other books include *Elegy for the Other Woman: New and Selected Terribly Female Poems, Tightening the Circle over Eel Country* (Great Lakes Colleges Association's 1975–1976 New Writer's Award winner), and *Raking the Snow* (Washington Writer's Publishing House 1981–1982 winner). She edited *The Dolphin's Arc: Endangered Creatures of the Sea. p. 73*

LYNN ROBBINS is a poet and graphic designer whose work focuses on helping women self-publish. Her career was reinvented five years ago when she discovered women's poetry and began writing and midwifing little books. Her poems have appeared in several anthologies and in the 1997 *Poet's Market. p. 50*

KAREN SANDBERG has published poetry in *Loonfeather, Blossoms & Blizzards*, and yearly editions of *Root River Poets*. She has been a registered nurse in obstetrics for twenty years at Rochester Methodist Hospital. Her two sons are grown, and her stepson is still growing. She lives with her husband on the bank of the Zumbro River. She grew up in an interesting house on the north shore of Lake Superior. *p. 167*

JOANNE SELTZER's work appears in four previous Papier-Mache anthologies. She lives with her husband and cat in Schenectady, New York, but wrote "Womanpower" at Act 1 Creativity Center in Lake Ozark, Missouri, which offered a room of one's own and mythic, mystic sunrises. *p. 123*

VERONICA A. SHOFFSTALL wrote "After a While" when she was nineteen. Now in her 40s, she is a Baha'i and plants her garden in New York City where she continues to write and to learn. "After a While" has appeared in several books, including Ann Landers's *Wake Up and Smell the Coffee*, as well as on refrigerator doors everywhere. *p. 103*

DEBORAH SHOUSE's parents told her, "Please do the write thing." And so she has been trying ever since. Although she now wonders, did they mean "right" or "write"? Her writing has appeared in *Reader's Digest, Newsweek, Redbook, Family Life, Family Circle,* and *Ms.* She coauthored *Working Woman's Communications Survival Guide* and *Still Following Her Star: The Donna Lee Story* and wrote *Breaking the Ice and Name Tags Plus. p. 104*

NANCY MCLAUGHLIN SIRVENT is a Boston-based writer and editor. "Runoff" is excerpted from her novel-in-progress, *Cahoots.* Her work has also appeared in *The Evergreen Chronicles. p. 15*

DONNA SPECTOR's poems, stories, and monologues have appeared in many journals and anthologies. Her plays have been produced Off Broadway and Off Off Broadway, regionally and in Canada. *p. 124*

SUNLIGHT left molecular biology to write full-time and left cities to return to the land and the trees. The author of *Womonseed and Being,* her stories have appeared in *Maize, Sagewoman, Sojourn,* and three anthologies: *Awakening, Mother/Daughter Voices,* and *Alternatives. p. 148*

EDWINA TRENTHAM teaches English at Asnuntuck Community Technical College in Enfield, Connecticut, and also teaches courses in women's poetry in the graduate liberal studies program at Wesleyan University. Her poems have appeared in a number of periodicals and anthologies. *p. 98*

JANET LEE WARMAN, originally from Richmond, Virginia, now teaches English and education at Elon College in North Carolina. Poetry and travel are her passions, and she is a devoted anglophile. Her poems have been published in about a dozen poetry magazines nationwide. *p. 81*

JESS WELLS's seven volumes of work include a new anthology, *Lesbians Raising Sons* (Alyson Publications), and a novel, *AfterShocks* (Third Side Press, U.S., and The Women's Press, U.K.), which was nominated for an American Library Association Literary Award. Her four collections of short stories include *Two Willow Chairs* and *The Dress/The Sharda Stories.* Her work has appeared in more than twenty literary anthologies within the lesbian, gay, and women's movements. *p. 109*

JOAN ZIMMERMAN, born in Britain, earned her doctorate in physics from Oxford University in 1971. Her travel articles on Tibet and Nepal have appeared nationally, most recently in *Travelers Tales Nepal.* Her poems are published in *Quarry West, Writing for Our Lives,* and *Coast Lines. p. 34*

I AM BECOMMING THE WOMAN I'VE WANTED
Becoming is the proud winner of a 1995 American Book Award for its representation
of American writing as culturally and ethnically diverse. This best-selling book focuses
on how women feel about their bodies and the broader question of how the physical
aspects of being female affect women's experiences.

*"Tending toward the emotive and always from the subjective, these pieces articulate what
it is like to be Everywoman from every age."* —LIBRARY JOURNAL

ISBN 0-918949-49-1, trade paper
ISBN 0-918949-50-5, hardcover

IF I HAD A HAMMER: WOMEN'S WORK
This insight-filled anthology explores women's methods of surviving in the workplace
in a variety of both traditional and nontraditional roles. *If I Had a Hammer* offers an
inspiring glimpse into women's shared feelings of empowerment and self-determination.

*"A remarkable collection that explores women's attitudes toward work...both literary and
documentary in its scope."* —BELLES LETTRES

ISBN 0-918949-09-2, trade paper

WHEN I AM AN OLD WOMAN I SHALL WEAR PURPLE
Winner of a 1991 American Booksellers Book of the Year Honors Award, *When I Am
an Old Woman I Shall Wear Purple* takes a refreshing look at the issues of aging in a
society that glorifies youth. These simple, compelling words share the universal
message of aging as a natural gift of life.

"You're not getting older, just a little more purple." —MILWAUKEE JOURNAL SENTINEL

ISBN 0-918949-16-5, trade paper
ISBN 0-918949-15-7, hardcover
ISBN 0-918949-83-1, large print

papier-mache press

At Papier-Mache Press, it is our goal to identify and successfully present important social issues through enduring works of beauty, grace, and strength. Through our work we hope to encourage empathy, respect, and communication among all people—young and old, male and female.

We appreciate you, our customer, and strive to earn your continued support. We also value the role of the bookseller in achieving our goals. We are especially grateful to the many independent booksellers whose presence ensure a continuing diversity of opinion, information, and literature in our communities. We encourage you to support these bookstores with your patronage.

We offer many beautiful books and gift items. Please ask your local bookstore or gift store which Papier-Mache items they carry. To obtain our complete catalog, mail your request to Papier-Mache Press, 627 Walker Street, Watsonville, CA 95076-4119; call our toll-free number, 800-927-5913; or e-mail your request to papier-ma@sprynet.com. You can also browse our complete catalog on the web at http://www.ReadersNdex.com/papiermache. To request submission guidelines for our next anthology, write to Papier-Mache Press, 627 Walker Street, Watsonville, CA 95076-4119, or visit our web site.